Advance Praises

"Nana Kyerewaa Opokuwaa continues her mission to help bring enlightenment to people of African descent. She is clearly one of the best spiritual coaches and teachers living today. Her insights, guidance and instruction in **Quest for Spiritual Transformation** is a seminal work on Akan Religion and Spirituality. The reader will simultaneously be educated, inspired and empowered to weave this important material into their life in ways that will continue to uplift a people in need of a refreshed spiritual protocol. If our roots, culture and history are critical to our human development, and it is, this important book is a must read for those who seek useful knowledge, divine wisdom and practical application. Thank you Nana Opokuwaa for sharing with us what the Creator has shared with you."

—**George C. Fraser, Author**
Success Runs In Our Race,

◆   ◆   ◆

Africans in the diaspora have been engaged in a 400 year journey seeking to find our way "back home." Only in recent years have we realized that the map that will take us back home to Africa is a spiritual map and requires navigation by the spiritual principles of our African reality. We appreciate the efforts of guides such as Nana Opokuwaa who have immersed themselves in the culture, in the spiritual path and have devoted themselves to helping us find the way. The Quest for Spiritual Transformation written by Nana Kyerewaa Opokuwaa is another of her valuable contributions to the road-map back home.

—**Na'im Akbar, PhD**
(aka Nana Owusu Nkwantabisa III)
Author, Lecturer, Consultant

◆　　　◆　　　◆

"…This book will become a classic. Not only is this a manual for spiritual practitioners and seekers, it can be a source for social workers, psychologists, teachers and any one who works with students or clients that suffer from "psychic trauma" from over 500 years of slavery. Thank you Nana."

—**Akosua Gyeaboa, MSW, LCSW**
(aka Okomfo Enyo Afriyie)

◆　　　◆　　　◆

"An important contribution to those re-connecting with traditional African religion and culture. It is clearly written, understandable as well as being quite engaging."

—**Nina Cadney, LGSW**
(aka Okomfowaa Nsia Korantemah)

◆   ◆   ◆

"This is a valuable book that will help all spiritual leaders and practitioners understand some of the similarities and differences between African religion, specifically the ancient Akan Akom Tradition, which is presently practiced in the Diaspora, and other mainstream religions."

—*Bishop Myles Spires, Jr.*
Abundant Life Ministries
Author, Come and Dine the Master Calleth

◆   ◆   ◆

As youth in search for a connection to our ancestors, this awe-inspiring book enlightens us about a culturally relevant spiritual system that will also nurture our personal development. Nana, thank you for taking us on this soul journey.

—*LaToya Spires*
Student, Drew University

The Quest For Spiritual Transformation

The Quest For Spiritual Transformation

✦

Introduction to Traditional Akan Religion, Rituals and Practices

Nana Akua Kyerewaa Opokuwaa

iUniverse, Inc.
New York Lincoln Shanghai

The Quest For Spiritual Transformation
Introduction to Traditional Akan Religion, Rituals and Practices

iUniverse books may be ordered through booksellers or by contacting:

iUniverse
2021 Pine Lake Road, Suite 100
Lincoln, NE 68512
www.iuniverse.com
1-800-Authors (1-800-288-4677)

ISBN-13: 978-0-595-35071-1 (pbk)
ISBN-13: 978-0-595-79777-6 (ebk)
ISBN-10: 0-595-35071-2 (pbk)
ISBN-10: 0-595-79777-6 (ebk)

Printed in the United States of America

This book is dedicated to the memory of my mother, the late Mrs. Ollie Mae Sharpe (nee Rucker), who made her sudden transition to the land of the Ancestors on February 16, 2004, while I was in Ghana writing a major portion of this book.

Contents

Preface

WISDOM KEEPING

From the late Nana Yao Opare Dinizulu, who was the first Okomfohene and Omanhene of Akans in America

Nana Says: "We must embellish our own culture if we are to be strong."
Nana says: "We must promulgate the culture."

◆　　　◆　　　◆

It is with these sayings in mind that I have attempted to write this book about ancient Akan religion which we call the Akan Akom Tradition, spirituality, rituals and rites of passage as I have experienced it over the past 17 years. It is a follow-up to my first book entitled *"Akan Protocol: Remembering the Traditions of Our Ancestors"* that was published a few years ago. This book is my continuing contribution and sharing of information about the ancient traditions and customs of the Akans of Ghana, West Africa and the teachings of the elders who have assisted me in my search for knowledge during these years.

As I travel to Ghana every year I find that, as in any profession, the more I learn the more I have to learn. I am Akan but I did not grow up on the Continent where an infusion of information comes just by observation and listening. Some of the information is given around the hearth. Some information is discussed in peer groups. Parents, grandparents and great-grandparents pass on important information when working, cooking, or storytelling. Information on any topic that needs to be told may be transferred through songs that are spontaneously sung at any gathering of people. We who were born in the Diaspora are at a disadvantage unless we spend an enormous amount of time and know some of the language that is being spoken in Ghana, our villages and towns. We will not be privy to the deeper insights about the culture, its history, the traditions and customs that are available if we are not patient and have a trusted interpreter.

However, if we should visit on a regular basis and participate in the religion in the Akan Akom Tradition, important ceremonies, the rituals and events that happen in the normal course of being there, we will gain a lot of knowledge about the culture. We become familiar with the customs and ways of our Ancestors. I find that it is possible to gain internal immersion in the culture that surpasses the romantic level that so many people tend to operate due to their inability to travel to Ghana often as participants rather than tourists. It is from this point of view that I write this introduction to this ancient system. I thank Almighty God, the Abosom and my Ancestors for providing me with the opportunity to learn and share the information that is appropriate for the masses who want to know.

This book is an *introduction* to the Akan Akom Tradition, an ancient religion that has its roots in Ghana, West Africa and is being practiced in other African countries as well as in the Diaspora. This book is born from the questions and comments of participants of the Asomdwee Fie, Shrine of the Abosom and Nsamanfo, Inc. (AFSANI) workshop which carries almost the same title. It also has its genesis in other pertinent workshops that I have conducted throughout the United States. Hopefully this book takes interested practitioners (and those who are seekers of more spiritual knowledge) of the Akan tradition another step towards receiving the benefits of a rich and great culture.

This important book emphasizes that the ancient Akan religion is not a separate part of life but gives structure to one's whole life. It further emphasizes the required reverence for and connection with ancestors and elders. It points out the strong connections of family and community. The book explains the importance of regular ritual and celebration. It emphasizes the necessity for effective rites of passage. Finally, and most profoundly, this book exhibits that the spirit of ancient Akan culture and religion could not be broken during the brutal Middle Passage and continued persecution of Black people throughout the Diaspora today.

I want to assure you that this is not a comprehensive look at traditional Akan religion, rituals, and practices. Rather, it is a survey of those important events that I feel comfortable in sharing and some of the knowledge that I have gained about each. I encourage anyone who is currently practicing or is interested in practicing traditional Akan religion to use this as another springboard to open the doors to a body of ancient rituals, customs, and practices rooted in Akan Spirituality and religion that will positively affect every part of your life. It is also a notable primer for those who are on a **Quest for Spiritual Transformation** in a system that they are able to identify as undeniably culturally relevant.

In addition to using books to study the ancient Akan religion, you must have an intimate experience and a teacher to fully understand and benefit from this system. Though it may be exciting and the temptation great, one cannot effectively practice this culture without proper initiation performed by a qualified Okomfo (Akan Priest) who has been properly trained in the tradition. It is not a self-initiating system.

Thank you for allowing me to share this information with you.

Peace and Blessings,
Nana Akua Kyerewaa Opokuwaa

Acknowledgements

Anyone who has written a book, attempted to write a book, or dreamed about writing a book knows that the journey from intentions to mind to paper can be very long. And, so it was with me for many reasons which all turned out to be somewhat invalid. I want to thank all of the members of AFSANI for your gentle and continuous encouragement that helped motivate me to write this book. As I began the mental and physical preparations for writing based on my first experience, I asked some of the members of AFSANI to write outlines of classes which they have become proficient in presenting in the workshop "Introduction to Akan Religion and Culture". They did a wonderful job in letting me know how much they have learned. So, Obrafo Kwasi Adhimu Baucum, Okomfowaa Ama Anum Yeboa aka Keisha Trotter, and Okomfowaa Yao Nson Barrington Salmon, medasi pii for your contributions to this work.

Thanks to all those unnamed Okomfo, Okomfowaa, and other Akan practitioners who have encouraged me by sharing their comments about the importance of the information provided in **Akan Protocol...**and the fact that they looked forward to the completion of this book.

Many thanks to the reviewers of this manuscript for the time, energy and support that you provided me to ensure the success of this book. To all AFSANI members, thank you for the various ways in which you supported me. Wo'fa Kwasi Odaaku, thank you for your understanding of this process and your overall support of my efforts.

To my daughter, Florentia M. Kavindama, thanks for the breaks that you insisted on me taking. To my granddaughter Wange, thanks for the polite and sometimes hilarious interruptions online, forcing me to take a deep breath. To my granddaughter, LaToya Spires, a great big thank you for your ongoing inspiration, comments, and enormous amount of assistance in the mechanics of preparing this manuscript. I love you girls!

Additionally, I wish to thank all the Akomfo in Ghana who helped me clarify various passages and shared pertinent information regarding the Akan Akom Tradition. To all of the Chiefs, Queenmothers, Akomfo and Bosomfo who allowed me to take pictures at their special events in Ghana to use as I determined appropriate to help spread the culture and religion in the Diaspora, a great big thank you.

To my Elders in Atonkwa, especially Nana Kodwo Eduakwa V, Chief of Atonkwa, Nana Kodwo Nyame, our Abusua Panyin, and Egya Ata, who provided me with stories and anecdotes about the religion and the culture. A very special thanks to my very good friend and confidante, Mr. Kweku Annan, for his patience, understanding, and the many ways that he assisted me as I labored with this manuscript in Ghana.

I want to give a great big thanks to my proofreaders, typists, formatters, and reviewers who labored tirelessly with me with a great amount of patience to "get it right". Ama Anum Yeboa (Keisha Trotter. Founder of Kee Concepts, A Web Design Company), who provided the initial format and indexing; designed my website; and kept my morale boosted. Thanks to Nkosi K. Ayize, Computer Graphics Technician, who patiently worked with me in the preparation of the photographs for publication. Nson Barrington Salmon, for the moral support and my introduction to the Editor, Ms. Joan Grant, thank you.

To all those very special friends and associates who freely shared opinions, comments, encouragement and prayed for me throughout this process, thank you.

Most of all, I thank Almighty God, Nana Asuo Gyebi, and Nananom who gave me guidance, confidence and motivation as I labored with this book. I could not do this work without their uncompromising and consistent encouragement and assistance. And, to my Ancestors, especially Uncle Bub, who kept whispering into my ear "You can do it!" I give honor and thanks.

Foreword

Kwa David Whitaker, Ph.D., Esq.
aka Nana Kwa Kra Kwamina, Tufohene of Atonkwa, Elmina Ghana

Over the course of the last two decades I have spent time on every continent with the exception of Australia and Antarctica. The purpose for these visits has been to make informal observations of the conditions and status of African descendants in their native land and throughout the Diaspora. After numerous trips abroad, including Africa, South America, Mexico, The Caribbean, West Indies, and numerous European Nations, I am convinced that African descendants have the dubious distinction of being 'second-class citizens' the world over!

This reality of subservience is especially glaring in those countries where Europeans dispersed Africans as a part of the dreaded 'Middle Passage'. The wholesale kidnappings, false imprisonment and unlawful transportation of African people represent crimes against humanity of a magnitude never witness in history—before or since.

European greed, economic opportunity and religious manipulation combined to create the diabolical forces that resulted in the forced migration of hundreds of millions of Africa's men, women and children. Today the descendants of these unwilling immigrants represent the world's largest group of displaced people living outside their indigenous homeland.

Oppressive psychosocial and economic systems combined with intense physical abuse, emotional trauma and cultural isolation to subject these 'New World" Africans to the most prolonged and horrific treatment imaginable.

What was the impact of this systematic mistreatment?

Even cursory research reveals many theories and hypotheses leading to the inevitable conclusion that the African Ancestors were victims of the most egregious terror and PostTraumatic Stress in human history. From the halls of academia to local barbershops many common elements emerge concerning the African's experience in the Diaspora.

One important theme is that Ghana's Akan represented one of the largest groups taken from West Africa's dreaded dungeons. The second is that the psycho-social and economic infrastructure required to wrench 'free labor' from the enslaved Africans was pervasive, continuous and dehumanizing. In North America the British colonist created and maintained a discriminatory system that was legalized and perpetuated by both state and federal agencies alike. With government sanctions this systematic terror persisted for nearly 250 years. The third, similar to recent Holocaust litigation and recent Reparations filings, is the presumption that the African Ancestors were abused and, as a result, their descendants continue to suffer losses.

If we accept the premise that the enslaved Africans suffered and their descendants continue to suffer, how would the appropriate characterization of their losses?

Some losses, those including the loss of family and friends, freedom of opportunity and the loss of property, are obvious. Others, like self-esteem, cultural identity/continuity, and racial cohesiveness, are subtle. In short, when translated into the 'American Dream' vernacular, the unwilling immigrants and their descendants were and, to a large extent, continue to be denied fair access to the pillars of American democracy—life, liberty and the pursuit of happiness!

If we agree that each of the foregoing represents a significant loss, there is, in my opinion, an even more significant loss that requires consideration and serious examination. Research reveals that African people, since deep antiquity, structured their existence around a comprehensive set of Spiritual constructs that enabled them to unlock the secrets of the universe, live productive, purposeful lives and leave a legacy of excellence that is without equal in the world today. Egypt's pyramids, among others, stand as a testament to this legacy.

Africa's reliance upon sophisticated Spiritual knowledge aligned with sound behavioral standards laid the foundation for civilized human interaction and represents—aside from people themselves—her most profound contribution to the forward progress of humanity.

The contemporary notion of Africans as a 'Spiritual people' is a direct result of their documented beliefs, practices and traditions. When viewed vis-a-vis the status of African descendants throughout the Diaspora, and most particularly in North America, our second-class status can be attributed to fact that we are a 'Spiritual people' without its true 'Spiritual identity'. Instead of engaging in an unrelenting quest for our lost Spiritual systems we have adopted hybrid and bastardized renditions of our own traditions with the naïve belief that they will somehow serve as useful tools.

Consequently, we journey from 'church-to-church', 'group-to-group' and leader-to-leader in a strange ritualized odyssey seeking answers to the age-old questions of Who am I? Where am I going? And. Why am I going there? The questions our Ancestors resolved centuries ago and, moreover, the answers to which have been left for us in their comprehensive set of Spiritual guidelines.

Absent our continuing Maafa (mass destruction) we would already possess this important knowledge and be utilizing the Spiritual practices—*still at our disposal*—to solve the problems confronting us as a people. Unfortunately, until we integrate true African Spirituality into our personal philosophy and daily practice, we will continue to wander through the confusing morass of religiosity—sampling from a meaningless smorgasbord of religions devoid of Spiritual sustenance.

Without important guidance this pointless odyssey will continue until our demise. A familiar proverb says "when the pupil is ready the teacher will appear'. Nothing could be more apropos to characterize Nana Kyerewaa Opokuwaa's ***Quest for Spiritual Transformation: An Introduction to Traditional Akan Religion, Rituals and Practices.*** Nana's style makes it clear that she appreciates the Spiritual deficiencies that exist in our people. She exhibits a special sensitivity and compassion for the reader's need for gentle and caring guidance as opposed to the heavy handedness that is often employed by other authors. Nana nurtures the reader's comfort by placing the material in a most user-friendly format.

At the outset Nana lays an uncomplicated philosophical foundation to show how the Akan conceptualized the universe and how they described the important relationship between the people, the Ancestors and the principle Deities. Nana proceeds to explain the step-by-step process by which we can establish and maintain a meaningful relationship with those that have gone before us. She also offers practical steps and uncomplicated rituals that we can perform to establish and maintain an open dialogue with our Ancestors.

Nana continues to build upon this foundation by introducing the reader to the Akom—the traditional Akan religious service. Here Nana goes beyond the customary brief introduction and shows us how to dress, the appropriate protocol, Akom behavioral expectations and important taboos while in the presence of Deities. Moreover, Nana explains the role of sacred songs, the dances and describes the Spiritual orchestra and its important role in the service. Nana continues by guiding the reader through an important discussion of the Spiritual hierarchy as well as the appropriate protocol in the event that a Deity or ordained Spiritual practitioner has been offended.

The final three chapters include an overview of some of the important Akan celebrations, sacred days, special rituals and 'rites of passage' practices that are considered vital to the maintenance of healthy individuals and viable communities. It must be remembered that, in the final analysis, the objective of an Akan life is to behave in accordance with socially acceptable norms, manifest the purpose for one's existence, strengthen the village/community, and provide proper guidance for children who will continue the Akan traditions.

As African descendants living in America we grow increasingly anxious about the future of our people. The more we hear "…things are getting bad and I worry for the children" the more we should be convinced that something is terribly wrong with society. The more our children die young, face long-term incarcerations and live out meaningless existences the more we should know that God could not have intended for this to be our destiny. The more we fail in our desperate search for answers the more we should realize that we are obviously looking in the wrong places!

As 'New World' Africans we have spent nearly 400 years employing myriad strategies to achieve the illusive 'American Dream'. Despite all our efforts we find ourselves on the proverbial square one at the dawn of the millennium. In many respects we are worse-off than our Ancestors who arrived aboard the Good Ship Jesus—at least they knew they were Akan, they knew their language, their Spiritual beliefs, practices, rituals, and important celebrations.

I am reminded of a quote that seems most appropriate to our Spiritual dilemma. It says "one is better off knowing where to go and not knowing how, than being free to go and not knowing where." Our Ancestors were unwilling immigrants who knew where to go—Africa—but they didn't know how. As their descendants, we are free to go but, after generations of indoctrination and cultural amnesia, we no longer know where...

As one who has been adrift for some time I feel a special sense of gratitude for Nana's recent offering on the Akan religious traditions. It is a perfect follow-up to her book entitled **Akan Protocol...**and serves as a most important 'beacon of light' that can guide our transformation towards our true spiritual center. If you are a conscious seeking African descendant I am confident that you will find it as useful as I have in navigating the troubling waters of daily life *a long way from home.*

Thank you Nana. Medawase! Medawase! Medawase!

Chapter 1

The Beginning: A Brief History of Traditional Akan Religion in the USA

In 1965, the late Nana Yao Opare Dinizulu I, whose grandmother's stories and subsequent research had revealed to him that his Ancestors came from Ghana, continued to make soul journeys to Ghana. After taking several trips to Ghana, in 1965 Nana Dinizulu was led to the Akonedi Shrine in Larteh, a town in the Akwapim region of Ghana. He received a Shrine consultation by the late Okomfohemaa Nana Akua Oparebea's mother. Nana Dinizulu was directed to his ancestral home through this divination. He was completely overwhelmed to find that the information revealed in his divination was true and consistent with the information he had received from his grandmother. According to accounts by his family, it was during this trip that the late Nana Dinizulu I was subsequently initiated as an Akan Priest. He was given the titles Omanhene and Okomfohene of Akans in America.

Through his divination in Larteh, the late Nana Dinizulu I was able to uncover a Shrine that had lain dormant for several decades. Upon his return to the USA, he brought back that newly discovered Shrine called Nana Kumi. He also brought back Nana Asuo Gyebi, Esi Ketewaa, and Adade Kofi Shrines.

In 1967, he established the traditional African religious and cultural organization, Bosum Dzemawodzi in New York. This organization continues to function today.

In 1971, the late Nana Dinizulu I requested, received and established the Akonedi Shrine in the U.S.A. It was during this time that he was recognized as the first to introduce Africans born in America (African Americans) to the Deities of Ghana, West Africa. He invited Okomfohemaa Nana Akua Oparebea to visit the USA and she accepted the invitation.

Once here, Nana Akua Oparebea established Nana Asuo Gyebi, Esi Ketewaa and Tegare Shrines in New York, Philadelphia, Washington, DC, California and Toronto, Canada. Many of those Shrines are functioning today. When returning to Ghana, she took young men and women for training at the Akonedi Shrine at Larteh. She taught Nana Dinizulu how to train Akomfo (traditional Priests and

Priestesses) to serve the Deities. The first line of Akomfo trained in the Diaspora began their training in 1971 under the tutelage of the late Nana Dinizulu I.

During the late Nana Oparebea's second visit to the US in 1972, she established additional Shrines and began the training of additional Akomfo. Since that time, many other Shrines and Deities have been brought to America by other Akomfo who were trained in Larteh, at other Shrines in Ghana, and by accomplished Akomfo in the USA.

We are acutely aware that the tenets of the ancient Akan religion were being practiced covertly in the Diaspora for hundreds of years. During slavery our Ancestors were not permitted to engage in religious and cultural activities without retribution by the slaveholders. So various means were designed to continue the most important components of the religion and culture without punishment. Most African Americans have heard stories from parents, grandparents and great grandparents of the practitioners in the South. In the '50s and early '60s there were outward movements of *Sankofa* (taking back that which was lost) by many revolutionary ancestors of African descent.

It must be recognized that the Late Nana Yao Opare Dinizulu I and Nana Akua Oparebea from Larteh were ultimately the most instrumental in the recognition and open practice of traditional Akan religion and culture in the Diaspora.

The Late Nana Akua Oparebea
Okomfohene of the Akonedi Shrine in Larteh, Ghana

The Late Nana Yao Opare Dinizulu, Omanhene
and Okomofohene of Akans in America.

Chapter 2

A Synopsis of My Understanding and Perspectives

If you have studied any African religion, you have clues to the Akan religion, because there is a common thread. If you have studied African cultural practices, you know about the religion because embodied in the everyday life of an African on the Continent and in the Diaspora, are rituals and ceremonies that are actually ancient religious practices. If you know something about African American culture and religion, you also know something about Akan culture and religion. Our Ancestors who were forcibly removed from the Gold Coast (now known as Ghana) brought with them the only thing that they could carry. They brought with them practices, which helped them to survive their tremendous ordeal, both in the Middle Passage and their ordeal of subsequent enslavement in the Diaspora.

People of African descent living in the Diaspora, had been cut off from their spiritual practices through slavery. However, the spiritual and cultural connections remained through proverbs, rituals, stories, and beliefs that have been passed on from generation to generation by great-grandparents, grandparents, and parents.

I certainly have memories of my Grandmother passing on to me those proverbs, sayings and warnings. Mama said: Don't go into the kitchen, don't mess with the food, and don't go around Daddy Ernest during that time of month. Go to bed when it is thundering and lightening, God is talking so be still. Don't put your hat on the bed, its bad luck. Don't open an umbrella in the house, its bad luck. Don't lay your pocketbook on the floor; you'll lose your money. Don't talk with food in your mouth, you will choke. Cover your head for church or any Spirit can enter you. If you make your bed hard, you have to sleep in it. A hard head makes a soft behind. Life is like a boomerang. Don't split poles. A whistling woman and a crowing hen, ain't no good. Don't' walk around the house or outside eating food, makes the house poor. When you take hair out of the comb, burn it or flush it…someone can get it and do evil with it. Or, the birds will get it, make a nest of it and that will give you bad headaches.

After Daddy Ernest made his transition, Mama insisted that at every meal a plate of food be placed on the table for him. This continued until she made her transition 15 years later. Many more sayings, Akan practices and traditions were taught to me by my grandmother. I remember her showing me the plants to cure a variety of sicknesses outside of her door. According to Mama, her mother (my great-grandmother) was a midwife and "knew plants." Momma was taught how to retrieve the plants at her mother's request. Her mother's mother (my great-great-grandmother) was a person that people came to for 'everything'. She was a Spiritual woman who could 'see' things and tell you what to do. My grand-mother's sister had visions, was born with a veil over her eyes. Mama was a prophetess in the Pentecostal tradition. My grandmother asked me to bring her a dress like mine. My reaction was "you won't wear it." It was then that she chal-lenged me saying her mother and grandmother and other women wore the same thing back then. She was referring to my African clothes…my lappas. Mama saw the marks on my arm and face and exclaimed, "You have your tribe marks. Let me see!" When I protested she said, "humph, that's nothing; everybody had them!" I suppose you can guess that the great matriarch had spoken and that ended my family's harassment about my African name and my chosen path! It was wonderful hearing these stories during her sunset years!

I am sure that everyone reading this book will remember many more "old folks sayings and practices" because the list goes on and on. This alone is an indi-cation that a reconnection to our spiritual inheritance is possible. The most inter-esting aspect of this to me, however, is that all of these sayings have similar Akan proverbs that were used by our Ancestors. The proverbs and practices can still be heard and seen in the traditional Akan household in Ghana.

This confirms for me that Akan culture and spirituality has been practiced in the Diaspora for a very long time. The major aspect lost was the ability to openly practice our ancient culture and speak our native language. We cannot minimize the affect that this had on us, even today. However, through the wise counsel and admonishments of our grandparents, and parents, elders, uncles and aunties, we continue to innately practice our culture in our homes and in public to a lessor degree. And, those who know and those who are not as aware might miss the signs. It is very important for the Elders today to continue to pass down what they know to the younger generation.

Yes, many customs were practiced secretly; however, many were buried and blatantly practiced in the churches right under the nose of those who thought they had annihilated a culture. If we look carefully, there are many parallels in rituals that are being performed in other major religions that are practiced in the Diaspora today. For example, a very important element of Christian faith is communion. As directed in the Bible, "Do this in Remembrance of Me." Communion consists of offering bread and drinking wine or grape juice accompanied by prayers. Each is blessed and then offered to all who wish to partake of it. Secondly, the act of communion creates a bonding of believers and participants within a common belief system. I encourage those who have a problem with Libation to carefully look at the parallel components of Libation. You will discover that actually there are similarities that hold true both with Communion and Libation, which are the same acts and intention but encased in different belief systems and customs.

Another great example of parallel beliefs is Okomfo Possession. Receiving the Holy Ghost is receiving the Spirit of God and the Ministers of God, as could only be ordained by God. All one must do is listen to the speaking in tongues and watch the Holy dance to understand that this is not an American, European, Portuguese or British custom, but a spiritual phenomena that could only be given by that Higher Power who we recognize as God. Likewise, look at the Okomfo Possession as described in this book. That too, is allowing the Spirit of God and the Ministers of God for whom we have names, to envelop the Okomfo. Subsequently, the spiritually possessed Okomfo performs the Holy dance and gives messages sometimes in a language different from their own. These things are displayed in a way that is not common to American ways and American knowledge.

Another great parallels are funerals, weddings and the language associated with these ceremonies. You will see the commonalities presented in this book. One could closely observe the customs associated with women in the Diaspora who lived with grandparents or older parents. When they are menstruating, custom dictates that they do not handle food, work in the kitchen nor associate too closely around the men in the family. In other words, these women are required to take a rest during "that time of the month." These customs have specific parallels in the ancient Akan culture.

Look at the head coverings and look at the gelee's and headdress of African-American women in church and at traditional ceremonies. Do they not lose their head coverings or hats when possessed by the Holy Spirit? Watch what happens to the Okomfo's head wrap or duku when the Deity gains possession. How many times do people "fall out" or are "slain in the Spirit" in church as compared to those who are slain in the Spirit at traditional Akan ceremonies only to get up and dance a good dance? Think of the music in church, currently and previously. The bass line is a facsimile of the drums that stir up the soul and call the Spirit down. An accomplished organist, pianist or drummer knows how to work up the so called "shout or holy dance," and conjure up or call down the Holy Spirit or Spirits or Abosom as we traditional Akans know them. We do not have to look far in other Protestant and Catholic churches to see the vestiges of our spiritual customs in the vestments worn by the High Priests in Catholic and Protestant churches that are white and other colors. We know that there is a connection between them and Africa. The specific colors and vestments worn by the High Priests and Priests during ceremonies are similar to those spectacular colors, robes and clothes worn in traditional African ceremonies.

Without continuing on this discourse, I want you to think about other customs that we have taken for granted and we have assumed come from a European background. We know that those customs and dress are taken from a culture much richer and older than that. They are directly connected to African people. It was easy to adapt our religious practices and hide them into the ceremonies that appear to be from the "so-called civilized countries". However, in Ghana as in some other African countries, increasingly more people get lost in the hoopla of the community. Social opportunities, as well as the pressing need for economic assistance in the form of used clothing and some other small handouts to children are also presented with these bogus copies of our ancient culture, religion and spirituality. Other religions have been introduced to "cultural sleepers" in a futile attempt to erase traditional religion from the minds and hearts of the people of African descent.

However, traditional religion cannot be separated from the culture and culture cannot be separated from ancient spiritual and religious customs. Traditional Akan religion is inseparable from every action and thought of an Akan. Akan people still embrace their spirituality...no matter how vigorously they might seem to pursue other religious courses or participate in other traditions, rituals and ceremonies. In the end, Akans continue to practice their indigenous religion.

Today, I am an eyewitness to the fact that many Akans who are staunch Christians, preachers, deacons, trustees, and choir members, still come to the Shrines for consultation. They sometimes come to participate in festivals, ceremonies and other rituals. So, if a Continental Ghanaian tells you that he or she does not practice traditional religion, you should interpret that to mean, "they don't practice all aspects of their traditional religion in the open." Engagements, marriages, naming ceremonies, funerals and other important rites of passage, as well as sacred days, are practiced routinely even though an additional ceremony may be performed in the church. Please know that even if done covertly, Akans must follow the traditions of their ancestors because they innately have a deep respect for what their ancestors can and will do to them, their family, or community for breaking ancient tradition. And, for those who don't? Well, custodians of the Shrines end up knowing about it.

Last year, as I was sitting in the family Shrine in Ghana, when a well known pastor entered the compound immediately after church…Bible and handkerchief in hand wiping the sweat off of his brow. He abruptly tried to hide the Bible because he did not immediately recognize me. This pastor was coming for consultation and additional traditional medicine. This was not the first time that I had witnessed him and other pastors coming into the shrine for assistance. It is a frequent occurrence.

Another story that was told to me by one of my Elders in the village was about this very subject of trying to hide traditional beliefs. A certain Reverend, who was preaching repentance and forgetting the old ways, died. When the church folks came to clean up the home, what do you think they found? A Shrine and everything that goes along with it, plus evidence of recent activity with the Shrine such as liquid in the pot, blood, feathers, bones, talisman and much more.

There are many other occurrences that I have personally witnessed that substantiate the fact that a 'modern' Ghanaian may outwardly practice another form of religion but will always return to his roots when real assistance is needed. Frequently, a person will go to the allopathic doctor, or hospital and finally the Native Doctor or Okomfo at the Shrines for rituals and traditional medicines. The allopathic doctor who may also be a traditionalist may subtly refer the patient to the Native Doctor. Studies show that more often than not, the person's health is restored after that visit, which may extend for weeks or months until the healing is complete. The Native Doctor takes the wholistic approach that investigates the spiritual, mental, emotional, and family as well as physical condition of the person.

In fact, traditional medicine is now being officially recognized in Ghana. Researchers at **The Centre for Scientific Research Into Plant Medicine** located in the Akwapim Region are studying the effectiveness of traditional medicines and techniques used by Native Doctors. They have currently substantiated the effectiveness of more than 50 herbs and formulas used by Native Doctors. The Centre is working with members of the Ghana Psychic and Traditional Healers Association as well as independent Native Doctors in order to confirm the use and healing properties of certain herbs. Many Akans believe that sickness occurs because they or a family member(s) has committed an offense against a Shrine or their Ancestors. Thus, they must go to a Shrine to seek help. Consequently, it is not uncommon for some to profess another religion yet still practice their indigenous religion in the face of adversities such as sickness or some other serious problem.

In my experience, some people believe that it is one or the other; that we must make a choice between Christianity or some other mainstream religion and traditional religion. It seems to me that those who are touting this belief really don't believe in the omnipotence of God who has created everything. In fact, this myopic view actually confirms their belief in a God who is limited in power. I strongly differ with that view. Actually, there is no real conflict, just a different approach. I encourage those who continue to misunderstand our ancient religion to study it with an open mind before continuing on this path of controversy, separation, and destruction. I believe that ultimately African people in the Diaspora and on the Continent will realize the truths and will make a choice of *Sankofa*!

In the meantime, it is important for African peoples in the Diaspora to embrace our indigenous culture and religion at least in increments until such time as we have the courage to integrate it completely into our daily lives. It is my opinion, that many in the Diaspora have not seized the opportunity to embrace the dress, religion, or customs of our Ancestors primarily because of economic reasons, peer and family pressures, or embarrassment. I ask the question of those persons who have written to me about this: What is the difference in the reasons we do not embrace our culture and that of our brothers and sisters on the Continent who some of us are claiming are "selling out" by practicing other forms of religion?

Do we remember that our Spirituality and religion was intact prior to any European, British or Portuguese peoples arriving in African countries? I remember that my grandmother despised the color Red. She said that according to the accounts of her elders, that is how 'they' tricked so many of our Ancestors by waving red silk cloth and offering them whiskey. She continued that "spices and other things were also offered".

Today, can't you see the comparison? I strongly believe that there should be no contradictions or competitions among the religious denominations if the various churches would only acknowledge that we are all from the same God and our basic Spirituality is from Africa. We all know that Africa has proven to be the first civilization according to the "scholars of today." Those who want to undermine the integrity of an entire culture have perpetuated the misconceptions of the indigenous African system of worship. It would be a wonderful occurrence if in this century we would no longer experience separation and begin to work together as one, acknowledge the truth thereby participating in the real growth, development and prosperity of Our People.

I believe that one answer to the Black man's dilemma of closed doors to opportunity; the Black woman's heavy burden of responsibility; our children's challenges to survive and succeed against all odds; the attempted destruction of our Black family; and the seemingly persistent designs to annihilate our race with drugs, alcohol, incarcerations, and poverty, is for all people of African descent who are living in the Diaspora, to reclaim our first spiritual birth right. We must participate in our African manner of worship to Almighty God, to acknowledge the presence of the Ministers of God or Abosom, and to recognize the contributions and on-going work of our Ancestors; which I believe will give us great assistance in continuing to ensure our survival in this land.

Under the direction of Almighty God, our Ancestors decided that we in the Diaspora needed some help here. They also looked at the sanctity of our religion and spirituality in light of what is happening in Continental Africa. They saw the need to preserve our traditions, culture and religion orally, in writing and in practice. This is why the Abosom, Orisha, Neteru, and other African Deities have decided to make an appearance in the Diaspora hoping that we would embrace religion and culture as much as possible. Hopefully, this will keep it in tact until such time as this violent revolution of trying to dismiss our African roots or being too embarrassed to acknowledge them is over. By all means, as the Elders say…**"what goes around will come around."** One only has to experience the attitude of many of the Continental Africans living at home and abroad to know that people of African descent who are practicing traditional customs in the Diaspora are playing a very important role in the survival of our traditional spirituality and religion.

Many of us in the Diaspora must come to terms with our own Spirituality. Many of us have searched for the "right" Spiritual connection. By all means, our Ancestors are continually trying to call us to our true inheritance. This happens to us through contact with other religions, reading cultural books, looking at metaphysical models, viewing websites on the internet, and on a more personal note, creating diverse situations in our lives that cause us to seek answers to dilemmas facing us. In the latter case, restlessness occurs and we wonder why. Our Souls, our Spirits, and our Ancestors are trying to get our attention. If we listen to that call, we find ourselves face to face with our African spiritual connection. This sometimes take years, and for some of the younger generation not as long since they are informed at an earlier age about our history. The educational system in urban cities has done much to connect our young people, eventhough that may have not been the intention. As we begin our "soul journey" a phrase that one U.S. Okomfo has coined, we ultimately run into the word "Akan" and thus are introduced somehow in someway to this ancient West African religion.

The Akan religion is orderly. We have a unique culture and religion that has its own Sacred Trinity which is comprised of Almighty God, who is the Creator of everything; the Abosom who are ministers and prophets of God, and our Ancestors who are the keepers of the culture and traditions. And, we the human beings are the beneficiaries of the powerful contributions they make toward our love, protection, health and care. Akans honor Almighty God and all of Her creation including the ministering Spirits living on another plane and the Ancestors. Human Beings are an extension of our Ancestors who are all a part of God's creation. We acknowledge that there are many entities working together to form a unified and ordered system of thought, movement, and existence to meet our every need.

If we study and follow the traditions of our Ancestors, we can better understand what is happening in our personal lives, our families and to some extent the world. Thus, Akan religion as practiced in Akan Akom Tradition is not an intellectual exercise. It is an expression of dependence upon a higher power not equal to man. This belief is expressed every day, in every action, in every word, and in every deed. It is believed that every action has a reaction. The living Akan proverb is "*If you do good to me, you do good to yourself; if you do bad to me, you do bad to yourself.*" It is taken very seriously in all aspects of life. We believe that you don't have to wait for rewards after you die, you get some things here on earth. You don't have to wait for punishment after you die, you or your family will be punished here on earth;...the law of Karma does exist. Individual destiny, ordained before you entered this plane, has a lot to do with those outcomes. In any event, honor, respect, discipline and honesty all share a prominent place in the life of the Akans. We believe in reincarnation. We try to live productive lives, which are worthy of our youth and others to emulate. We are then able to become Ancestors who are allowed the opportunity to assist those family members that we leave behind.

Chapter 3

PHILOSOPHY AND THEOLOGY

The Creation

An elder, who continues to practice traditional Akan religion, told me this story. Odomonkama, The Creator, first made the sky and then the earth, rivers and plants. Finally, he (she in creation) created man and animals. The animals fed on the plants already created and in turn provided the food for man. Man also needed protection in his environment and for this, God created the Spirits of the waters, forests and rocks. Then God created whom we call the lessor gods, the Abosom, to take care of man. Everything was created in order and every creature has its place and its special or particular function. In fact, the Akan proverb says, *Since God does not like fraud, God gave each creature a name."* God is still creating new wonders such as plants, babies, tributaries to rivers and more.

Akan religion does not entertain the concept of the original sin. To my knowledge there is no Adam and Eve story. Man was not born in sin. Quite the contrary. An Akan proverb says: "All that God created is Good." Everything that God created and placed on this earth was good. It shows that God continues to care and have compassion for all of his creation.

The Separation

An elder told me this story; she has since made her transition. I have heard the story many times since. There was a time when God and man lived on this earth very close…like a family. Our Ancestors could actually touch, reach and feel Him. They were very comfortable and dependent on Him for they could go directly to Him for whatever they needed. And, they needed Him for everything. They knew that they were not self-sufficient. A particular old woman loved to stand close to God every day. And, everyday while standing close to God, and when it was time for her to eat she cooked her soup and pulled over her traditional mortar and pestle to pound her fufu. Each time she pounded her fufu, without fail she would accidentally hit God. God moved over so as not to get hit. The next day she would come back to be with God again and the same thing would be repeated. She would pound her fufu using the traditional mortar and pestle and accidentally hit God again and again. God would move over a little more. Then he gradually started to move up and out of the old lady's range of motion. By and by the people realized God had moved so far out of her reach that no one could reach, feel, or touch him. So, of course, the people panicked. They got their heads together and decided to bring all of their mortars to build a ladder so that they could reach God. Well, everyone brought their mortars and began to build this ladder. By and by they discovered that they needed just one more mortar to make the ladder high and long enough to reach God. The old lady had an idea…if they would remove the bottom mortar and place it on top that surely would be enough. When they attempted to do this the whole ladder collapsed on them and many of the people were killed. Thus, they were no longer able to reach, touch or feel God in that way. However, they were aware of their need to do so because they knew that they were not self-sufficient. They had the experience and they needed to be in harmony, in unity and in touch with the Creator.

The Separation: Illustration by Malandala Zulu

God saw the predicament and grieving of the people. In His compassion, he created a system by which we could be in constant contact. It is through this experience that the tenets and methods of our ancient Akom tradition became a living and breathing practice. There are many versions of this story about our Ancestors on this particular topic but not one single name is mentioned or associated with the establishment of the Traditional Akan Religion. This myth and associated stories vary according to tribes, regions, villages, and communities but all have the same common thread running through them. God in His infinite wisdom and compassion created a mechanism by which we could reach him.

So, as you can see there was a Concept of God long before the invasion of missionaries and plunderers arrived in Africa particularly Ghana. Further, we believe that God is so great and so far above His Creation that when referring to Him, we do so by using appellations describing His attributes. I have listed ten (10) appellations however there are many more.

Appellations for God

Onyame, Nyame	To be Satisfied; Who alone is the Great One
Onyankompon,	
Nana Onyakompon	Grandfather
Twereduampon	Twere...lean; dua...tree;...mpon...bend not Thus, the tree that never bends nor breaks!
Odomankoma	Creator
Oboadea	The Creator
Nana, Paapa	The most important Grandfather, The Grand Ancestor
Awurade	Our Lord, Our Master; the One Who serves
Amosu	Giver of Rain
Amowia	Giver of sun or light
Nyamenekosa	The One In Whom I can confide

The Supreme Being

By tradition, Africans on the Continent have a firm belief in the Supreme and Almighty God. So it is with those of us in the Diaspora who follow the Akan Akom Tradition which is indigenous to Ghana, West Africa and is also found in Ivory Coast, Togo, the Congo, the Caribbean as well as here in the United States. Akans believe that God is the Supreme, self-existent being in whom all things begin and end, upon whom all things are dependent. Akans believe that God is everywhere but also far away beyond the reach of humans. **An Akan proverb states:** *No one shows the Supreme Being to a Child.* Meaning that the child lying on his back sees the sky, which is believed to be the abode of the Supreme Being. It is on the basis of this experience that our Ancestors came to the knowledge or conviction of the existence of a Supreme Being. Part of this experience is the awareness of our own our mortality. Conversely, the Supreme Being never dies.

Despite this firm conviction, the traditional Ghanaian does not worship God directly. Nana Onyankompon as we sometimes call Him, shows that He is the only true One, the creator of heaven and earth who also made the sun and gives the rain; omnipotent, omnipresent, omniscient and more. He is Supreme over all in an absolute sense. His authority cannot be questioned by any one. God is too unique. As previously stated, we know Him by many appellations such as Atwediampon, Okokroko, Onyame, Awurade, Oboadee, the Creator, Odomankoma-the One who can give us grace, Nyankopon, Asase Yaa-Mother earth, pure, unpolluted, motherly, protective, fruitful. He is the Great one, the dependable One, Eternal, Infinite, the Mighty of Mighties, transcending everything, able to satisfy, Egya-our Father, Awurade-our Lord, Ohene-our King, our Judge.

An Akan proverb states: *If you want to say something to God, say it to the winds.*

The Abosom

Besides the Supreme Being, we believe that there exists in our world a world of Spirits We believe that Spirits are everywhere. The Supreme Being is the Father and Creator of those Spirits. We sometimes refer to them as the Children, messengers or agents of God. They receive their powers from God. They are created by God to fulfill specific functions and did not come into existence on their own volition. Odomankoma knew that we would need help, that we would need a presence that we could see, feel and touch. So He created the Abosom specifically for us Humans on earth. There are the major, more popular Spirits or Abosom and there are smaller or less popular Spirits who are found all over Ghana. Nevertheless, all of the Spirits have powers given to them by God. However, their power is limited; Onyame's power is unlimited!

We believe that the Abosom are ministers or agents of the Supreme Being. They are known as the lesser gods, in that they have no power unto themselves but the power is from the Supreme Being. They however, are able to work independently, healing and protecting the people who worship them. They do not have dominion over life and death. That is reserved for Onyame. These Spirits have a generic name which is different from the names given to the Supreme Being. They are called Abosom (plural) or Obosom (singular) and sometimes are referred to collectively (along with the Ancestors) as the Deities.

Those Spirits are embodied in the wind, rivers, oceans, streams, trees, mountains, rocks, animals, and other inanimate objects. These objects of nature are not Spirits, but have Spirits living in them. They may either roam about or be quiet, but take up residence inside of natural forms.

These Deities are found everywhere in Ghana, even in the smallest communities, towns, and villages. They are male and female, or may have the power to embody both. The benevolent Spirits form a major part of our traditional religion. There are Abosom at traditional levels, clan levels, house levels and individually. They range from tribal gods to community gods or gods of families, to individual or private gods. However, they were never in human form living on this earth. They are placed well above humans beings each having his/her own area of expertise. They are not in conflict with each other; rather they complement each other in various ways. Their main objective is to create harmony and peace, so they work in harmony with each other.

Through the Abosom, we receive blessings, prosperity, protection from all dangers, difficulties, calamities and challenges of life, bodily and spiritual protection of our family. They bless the people with children, health and long life; reveal secret and future occurrences; diagnose diseases and prescribe their antidotes; strengthen people Spiritually, forecast the outcome of encounters; turn evil destiny into good destiny. The role of the Abosom in the traditional Akan religion, therefore, is great!

The number of Deities varies widely and there is also a difference in the identity of the Spirits. Some say there are at least 77+7 in each region of Ghana; plus the same number in towns, villages, community and family Deities. They have influence on human life and have to be reckoned with by man. When a community or family is experiencing challenges or are embarking upon something important, the Deities are first consulted. People are related to God through the Abosom. Abosom are intermediaries and immediate objects of worship. They are regarded as certain aspects of the manifestations of the Creator.

In Ghana, there are many Abosom, some rated very high, well known, well organized, very popular, effective and flourishing; others are similar to this group that is being mentioned but may not be as well known. They are male or female and sometimes are able to manifest as both. The sex of the Okomfo is not necessarily an indication of the sex of the Deity he/she is carrying. However, all the Deities that appear are highly respected for the works that they have been commissioned by Onyame to perform. When displaying or appearing to the public they wear clothes specific to their character and carry specific implements. They also wear ahenies or sacred beads which represent their system. It is impossible to list all of the Deities but I feel it necessary to mention a few who are popular in the Diaspora.

I have named Deities, which reside across several regions in Ghana. They may also reside in areas that I have not named or may be called by a different name. Thus I ask that readers consider this a sample of the Deities in Ghana. It is impossible to list all of the Deities in each region but it is important to mention a few who are popular in the Diaspora and Ghana.

Asase Yaa is also known as Mother Earth, Aberewaa, the Ol' Lady who is recognized as the nurturer of the earth provides sustenance for us all. She is called in our libations immediately after God. She cannot be compared to any of the other Deities. Asase Yaa does not have priests or priestesses. However, there are very specific taboos and qualities associated with her. The day set aside for Her is Thursdays. For Akans, there is no farming, no planting, and no burying the dead. This day is very sacred. To break any of these taboos is similar to *heaping coals of fire on your head*…for sure trouble is coming. She abhors spilling of blood, therefore sacrifices are made to her when a person is in an accident, or a person is killed. She upholds the truth and people who swear they are telling the truth are challenged to touch the tip of their tongue with soil which is akin to people in the Diaspora swearing on their mother's or grandmother grave. Before you dig in the earth, it is best to ask permission and pour libation.

Nana Akonedi, Abena Akonedi, or simply Akonedi. Her shrine is at Larteh Kubease, in a Sacred house, sacred groves and sacred streams. The Akonedi House is a well organized and controlled system of worship. She is known as Nana Panyin or the Ol' Lady throughout Ghana. She metes out justice and gives the final decision in difficult disputes related to chieftancy, heirarchy, property, land, family and other major issues. Due to her importance in the pantheon, she has few priestesses as compared to other Abosom. She appears very stately in white attire and carries with her the Akomfena and Broom which she uses in final judgments. Her Ahenies are all white. She displays early morning and does not stay around for a long time. Her presence and dance is graceful and cannot be mistaken for any other Deity.

Nana Asuo Gyebi is an ancient river Deity originally from Northern Ghana. He is very important to the Diaspora because **Nana Asuo Gyebi stated that "he came to the United States to help the lost children of Africa reclaim their Spiritual past."** His priests were among the first to be initiated in the United States. Nana Asuo Gyebi is a great healer and protector. It is said that he takes messages to the Council of Abosom to get answers when they are not easily forthcoming. Thus, he deals with the very difficult cases. Nana Asuo Gyebi is the Obrafo to Nana Panyin. Therefore, you cannot take his actions for granted. He displays in outfits of various colors and style including those originating from the Northern area of Ghana. However, his ahenies are red and white. His wives (and he has many wives) may wear a raffia or cloth skirt or lappa of the color of their choosing, and a white top lappa. He carries a bodua (sheep's tail) and a siekine (knife).

Nana Asuo Gyebi is known as a great dancer who in addition to his own dances is often seen dancing to the multi rhythmic sounds of Ghana high life. He is a statesman and Nana Asuo Ggyebi carries himself in that manner. He resides in a river in Larteh.

Nana Asuo Gyebi displaying the Bodua and Sikeine

Nana Esi Ketewaa Blessing A Child

Nana Esi Ketewaa in ancient times actually lived in the Akwapim area of the Eastern Region of Ghana. She is remembered as a very kind, gentle, generous person who was well loved by all who knew her. She was one of the Elders at the Akonedi Shrine in Larteh. It is said that Nana Esi became pregnant in her sunset years and died in childbirth. She was given the distinct honor of becoming a deified Ancestor. Nana Esi is now the Okyeame or linguist of the Akonedi pantheon's Council of Elders. Thus, she is able to bring messages directly from Nana Panyin to other Abosom. She is a peacemaker and is often called upon in that capacity. Throughout Ghana, women seek Nana Esi's medicine during pregnancy, delivery and after childbirth. She is well known as a protector of children.

Oftentimes, after Nana Panyin displays Nana Esi will appear to continue with messages and dance. Similar to Nana Panyin, Nana Esi does not display for a long period of time. Nana Esi has a stately appearance. She is very colorful and neat in her attire. Nana Esi wears a duku (head scarf) and dukus on her arms. She carries one in each hand. The colors are her choice. She wears a formal entoma over a top and bottom lappa. Nana Esi is a particularly graceful dancer. Her carriage is very maternal, nurturing and quite sophisticated. Her ahenies are white with black seeds. Nana Esi loves sweets such as candy, cookies, cake, honey,

Fanta orange soda and fruity wine. She also enjoys chicken, rice, and gin. Nana Esi possesses female Akomfo only.

Nana Adade Kofi is a male Bosom of strength and perseverance. He is the Obosom of iron, metals and is a fierce warrior. Adade Kofi is the youngest of Nana Panyin's children. He is also an Obrafo but is better known as an impatient messenger who is quite fiery. When Nana Panyin has a stern message such as *the last warning,* she will send Adadi Kofi to deliver that message. Most people are quite nervous when he appears; particularly if they have ignored some important message that was given during a previous consultation or otherwise. Adadi Kofi wears all white but not in the same fashion as Nana Panyin. Sometimes he wears a white skirt with or without color. He carries a sekiene and sometimes an Akokofena. True to his character, his dances are very fast and executed in quick elaborate and mostly complicated steps. He loves to dance and sometimes appears just to display his dances. Adade Kofi is not to be played with or bargained with. He is absolute in his messages. Only Nana Panyin can reverse his admonitions. So, His messages cannot be taken lightly. Adade Kofi wears an iron chain around his neck, leg and arm. He also often appears immediately after Nana Panyin leaves. Adade Kofi likes raw rice, gin, palm wine and all that Nana Panyin eats.

Tegare is the general name for a system of Deities from the northern section of Ghana. Nana Tegare is a hunter, who seeks truth, exposes witches, liars, thieves and evil doers. Nana Tegare lives in the forest as hunters do. He is a loner of sorts and is known by many other names. He is always watching to see who is honestly doing good work. When he comes, he wears the clothes of a northerner, batakari, short pants and hat. Tegare carries an Akonti, which is a hunter's stick. Nana Tegare is a great dancer who dances highlife. Most people love to see him appear as he usually arrives in great Spirits full of laughter and fun. People join in singing his songs and dancing with him. He enjoys dancing as much as Nana Asuo Gyebi who is his father. Nana Tegare arrives specifically to investigate the space, expose liars and evil doers. He often exposes underhand work when he displays. Many hear his jokes but one must remember that there is always a hint of truth in his words and laughter. There are many other Deities in this system of Tegare. One must be initiated to the system to know all of the Deities. He may carry Muslim prayer beads, wears ahenies, which are varied in color, and wears a whistle, which he constantly blows. The main identifier of Tegare is the Akonti.

Tegare Abosom-Ba

Nana Obo Kwesi is a war Obosom who is known in the Central Region of Ghana. He assists with the need for money and abhors evil doers. Nana Obo Kwesi wears war clothes in red and other colorful attire. He is a quick dancer and loves to dance. His appearance is usually limited in that he does not stay around a long time. He comes, dances, and gives messages and leaves. Through his dances and messages, there is no mistake that he is a warrior.

Mmoetia is a system of Spirits who sometimes appear as dwarfs or giants. They specialize in working with nature Spirits for healing body, mind and Spirit. They are considered the Spiritual gatekeepers of the traditional Akan religion. They are excellent herbalists and other Deities often work with them for special cases.

One of the most popular subsystems within Mmoetia is known as Nkwatia Kwatia. They are considered to be mischievous, playing so called tricks on those persons they decide to protect or interact with. However, in most cases they are trying to get your attention. For example, you might continuously lose your keys because you are not paying attention to details; you might continually trip over a particular thing because it is not in your best interest to have it in that location, and so on.

The Dwarfs are quite possessive. If they really like you, they will make their presence known in your life. Sometimes you will see them or think you see them. If you are eating and have not first offered them food, by all means, you will drop your food or spill your drink. They like order and if things are out of order they may inflict punishment on the person(s) who are responsible. This can often be seen at Akoms. The Dwarfs are great dancers and dance to all songs and rhythms. They dress in various clothing...not one type of dress is prescribed to the dwarfs. Most Deities have Dwarfs attached to them. So the attributes described for Nkwatia Kwatia is for all dwarfs with variances specific to the system that they are working in.

Nana Asuo Botopre is an ancient male deity from the Ashanti region of Ghana. He is a protector and healer. However, he is a warrior and carries implements used at war. He is usually dressed in a white cloth and raffia skirt. His holy day is Wednesday and his sacred ahenies are red and white. Some of his favorite foods are raw rice, sugar cubes, Fanta orange soda, fried fish, fried plantain, white yams, fowl, and bananas.

Nana Kumi is an ancient war Deity from Aburi-Nsaba, Ghana. He gives strength and fortitude. His shrine was found in 1972 by the late Nana Yao Opare Dinizulu I, after being dormant for many decades. Nana Kumi carries a bodua, knife as well as a spear at times. His sacred ahenies are reddish-brown, blue and white. He also wears a chain. He likes guinea fowl, schnapps, tiger nuts, white yams and turkey.

Nana Densua Yao is a river deity from the Akwapim area in the Eastern region of Ghana. He loves and protects children. Densu Yao drinks a lot as a result of a disagreement with his brother. He loves and protects children who love to dance with him. Whenever he displays, he will ask to pour libation for the children before he leaves. During the course of this libation, he is known to sneak a drink. Densu Yao wears a full colorful entoma and may carry a bodua. He is one of the principal elders at the Akonedi Shrine. He enjoys duck, rice, any type of liquor, and fruit.

The Nsamanfo (Ancestors)

Akan Proverb: *"The eye which saw the past is not living, but the ear, which heard what was said in the past (still) lives."*

(Explanation of proverb: Even though there is no one in the present generation that saw the past, we still remember the traditions of the Ancestors. The traditions have remained as each generation passed on what it heard to the next.)

The Ancestors form an important part of the Traditional Akan religion. They actually walked in human form on this earth. The Ancestors are also known as the Nsamanfo or Old People or Ancient People. They have a prominent place in the thinking and religious practices of our people.

Akans believe in life after death, therefore when a person's body dies their Spirit lives on not on earth but in their own land called "Asamando". The Ancestors are feared. At the same time, they are loved and respected; they are believed to be everywhere; they continue to live another kind of existence after their death; and their importance comes after that of the Supreme Being and Asase Yaa.

With all their importance, the Nsamanfo are not worshiped. They are venerated—veneration being a higher form of respect and honor. They remain the relatives of the living and are referred to by the same name or title that was used when they were alive. They are not approached as gods or Abosom. They are given a status level that is above the level given to any human. The Nsamanfo (Ancestors) are honored and appeased because they have acquired some of the power of the Abosom and are forever watching and protecting us. They are deemed to have gathered wisdom through the highly esteemed life they led while on earth and although absent from this life, they are believed to be concerned about what is happening here on earth within their families.

The Nsamanfo are in close contact with the Supreme Being whose favor they enjoy in a special way. Some enjoy the privilege of being deified Ancestors an honor bestowed upon them by Odomankoma. This means that they enjoy the same privileges as the Abosom who are assigned specific areas of responsibility. One of those Ancestors is Nana Esi Ketewaa who was discussed in the previous section.

Ancestors intervene between human beings and the Supreme Being, Nyame. Every individual has Ancestors particular to their family (whether we knew them in our lives or not) who are responsible for the protection, care and guidance of the remaining members of the family. We can call on them for assistance. However, if we do not adhere to family customs and traditions, or if we stray away from those established ways, they can cause havoc in our personal life, family and community. They are the custodians of the laws, customs and traditions of our society. Hence, we abide by their laws in the food we eat, our choice of dress, our hygiene and cleanliness, the way we raise our children, and our method of worship. Since respect is a major tenet of Akan culture, we are obligated to teach our children to respect our mothers, fathers, elders and even their peers. This is a major case for grievance and retribution by our Ancestors.

Our Ancestors are remembered and revered in many ways. Many people set up Ancestral Altars in honor of those family Ancestors. Rituals are performed to establish and maintain constant contact with our Ancestors to seek their guidance, direction, and in some instances needed comfort. We name children after them. We invoke them in rites and in ceremonies. We pour libation and make offerings to them. One of the most important ways in which our Ancestors are venerated is through the many festivals that we perform in Ghana and in the Diaspora. We celebrate Akwasiadae in 40-42 day cycles. It is always on a Sunday; however, it has nothing to do with Christianity. In recent years, however, the church leaders in Ghana plan important church activities on Akwasiadae. Every Akan family also sets aside this day to celebrate their family Ancestors in special ways.

Everyone who dies is not recognized as a revered or distinguished ancestor. Only those who meet the criteria as judged by the Supreme Being are permitted to enter the land of Asamando. Those criteria are having attained old age, which Ghanaians highly respect; productivity in the community, having gained a certain amount of wisdom through their lifelong experiences, and most importantly, having birthed children or had the responsibility for the upbringing of children

With all of the situations in the Diaspora, many questions have been asked about the Spiritual status of those who have died other than by natural causes. I would like to share with you the 3 categories of Ancestors as acknowledged by the Elders in Ghana. However, Almighty God reserves the right to give life or death and therefore also makes the ultimate decisions about Ancestors. There are rituals and ceremonies performed to ensure that a person is not stuck between two worlds…that of the living and the dead. Those rituals involve special libation, sacrifices and other ritualistic actions. Those rituals are conducted by the traditional Priests and Priestesses at the request of loved ones.

Saman-paa means an ancestor who died a good death such as naturally from old age 70 or more or an old age related sickness. Another type of death in this category is an honorable death by violence such as war or riot. The deceased was known as mother or father, meaning that they either had natural children or were responsible for the raising of children. Other criteria for this category is that the departed were known to do outstanding work in the family, society or community and therefore earned the name of mother or father. We name our children after Saman-paa. It is a great honor to be named after a distinguished Ancestor.

Saman-twen-twen, is an ancestor who never left the earth and shows up someplace else roaming about, or people report sightings of these spirits. They are stuck between two worlds. These ancestors have somehow lost their way to the land of the Ancestors. The soul simply refuses to leave the earth; they are stuck between two worlds. Special sacred rituals must be performed to force them to leave the earth and travel toward Asamando.

This is one of the reasons we believe that it is very important to conduct the proper burial and funeral with associated rituals for the deceased. These rituals continue for one year after the death of the person. We believe that the Spirit of the deceased stays very close to family and loved ones for 8 days before beginning to travel to the land of the Ancestors known as Asamando. For forty days the travel continues and the Spirit crosses that river of life on the 40th day. We perform 40 day rites for the departed. On the 80th day, the Spirit has reached Asamando and rites again are performed. The final rites are performed for one year. The Ancestor is then remembered at least annually when libation is poured.

Tofo is a deceased who experienced a violent death such as in a lorry or automobile accident, or drowned at sea. The main characteristic is that the persons body could not be recovered therefore the rituals have to be performed in order to summon their soul home so that proper burial and funeral rituals can be performed. Also, this category includes someone who committed suicide, or was electrocuted as well as persons who died with a serious incurable disease such as AIDS, cancer, and leprosy.

Building Your Ancestral Altar

If we believe that our Ancestors have more power and are able to assist us, and if we believe that they are tracking our family insofar as what we do in this world, and that they can reward or punish us, we must establish communication with them. If we plan to ask them to be intermediaries for us, and if we plan to ask them for assistance, we must establish communication with them. The ancestral altar allows us to establish that communication with our personal Ancestors in a real way. We can touch the altar, and feel the presence of those ancestors while we sit there, and talk there. It is our very own connection to those Ancestors who can help us. It is not to be shared with anyone else including relatives, spouses, significant others or children. This is very personal and private space. If you wish to establish a family altar then do so in an open space, perform a ritual, and introduce each person to the Ancestors at that altar as those who will be calling them for help. It is at this time that you may include everyone in the household.

Many of us have already acknowledged our Ancestors on different levels. We have visited the gravesites of our loved ones and left flowers. We have poured a drink on the ground before we consume the drink. We buy flowers to celebrate the birthday of a loved one who is deceased. We discuss the attributes and accomplishments of a particular ancestor whom we wish our children to use as role models. There are national holidays in which we participate to acknowledge our personal Ancestors as well as community Ancestors. Now that we have a more in-depth understanding of the importance of acknowledging our Ancestors, we have an opportunity to formalize this process even further by building our own very personal ancestral altar in our homes.

I am often asked how one should set up their ancestral altar. Your ancestral Altar is a very personal and sacred space. It is up to you to provide the setting that is most comfortable and appealing to you and in line with the wishes of your Ancestors. You will find that as you decide that you want to set up an altar, your Ancestors will begin to communicate with you. Perhaps you might think that it is your imagination, however it is definitely your Ancestors acknowledging your earnest desire to communicate with them. Thus, they begin to start providing input to your process. In any event, there are a few standard items that are necessary to use in setting up an ancestral altar.

Table. A simple table will be needed to hold the necessary items. For my first ancestral altar, I used 2 cinder blocks, placed a wide white shelf on that and covered it with white brocade cloth. You can also use a crate or two and set a wide shelf on top. Cover with a white cloth. You can find the shelf in the shelving section of a hardware supply store. Any type of table that you prefer is acceptable. Round, octagonal, rectangle…your choice.

A candle. I prefer a white candle which is often used in conjunction with ceremonies for the Deities. I believe it helps to pull in the Spirit of the Ancestors. The candle can be any size or any shape. Place the candle in something that will not burn, as you will be using this candle often. You will also need stick matches to light the candle.

A Libation Bowl. You will use this 1 quart bowl as your libation pot so it needs to be able to hold liquid. This bowl should be white. It can be a type of flower pot or a cookie jar with a top or white canister with a top that will allow the water to stay inside. This type of pot is easy enough to find in a home supply store in the flower section or in the kitchen section in any all-purpose store. If you purchase a flowerpot, also purchase a plate or saucer large enough to cover the top. The bowl should contain spring water over which you will pray and invite your Ancestors to come when you call them. Subsequently, you will pour libation into that sacred water whenever you desire. This will be placed on your table in a sacred, private and comfortable space, (i.e., in a corner, closet, special room or the special place in your home.)

Glass. You will need a whiskey shot glass to pour libation.

Bell. You will need a small bell to place on the altar to use when you summon your Ancestors as you pour libation.

Drinking Glass. You will need a drinking glass, goblet, or other type drinking glass to keep water in for your Ancestors. You can also fill this glass with soda or other beverage periodically for your Ancestors.

Fruit/Food Plate. It is customary that fruit, candy, cookies and sometimes a special meal can be placed on this plate periodically. It should not be larger than a regular plate. The color of the plate is your choice.

Vase. You may periodically place flowers on the altar for beautification. This is your choice but do not overpower the space.

Incense Holder. The Ancestors like sweet scents. Burning very nice incense periodically is a good idea. You may also use the incense of your choice.

Florida Water or Perfume. The Deities love sweet and distinct scents. In the African Spiritual religions, typically Florida water is used. In addition, you may use perfume if you so desire.

Pictures. You should place a picture of your ancestor on the altar. Pictures of Ancestors should not contain pictures of living persons included in them. You may have more than one picture on the altar. However, your primary ancestor or Spirit guide, the one you knew or resonate most with, should be most prominent with other Ancestors surrounding it. If you do not have pictures of Ancestors, write their names on a nice piece of paper and frame it. If you don't know of any of your Ancestors, just write on a piece of paper *For My Personal Ancestors*, and frame it.

This altar is for family and not community Ancestors. If you want to honor community Ancestors, I recommend that you set an altar for community Ancestors separate from your family Ancestors.

As you gather the items and place them on the table, be careful not to have a cluttered space. Say a libation and invite your Ancestors to the space informing them that you will be coming there periodically to talk. Again, this is a personal altar and placing it in the path of anyone entering your house is inappropriate. Having a stranger or friend's energy on your altar is not the best idea. If your altar is in an open area, I recommend that you use a white cloth to cover your altar except when you are there to pour libation, place food, or talk.

A Personal Ancestral Altar

Performing Rituals For Your Ancestors

Akan Proverb: "It is the living who make the inhabitants of the Spirit world long for the mashed yam."

It is up to you to design your own rituals for your Ancestors. The first ritual is to set up the altar giving it your full time and attention. Then pour libation in the bowl to invite your Ancestors there whenever you call them. Talk to them; sing to them, and do whatever you feel the need to do. Let them know that this is your special place to consult with them. You should decide which drink to use based on what your ancestor liked, or perhaps you may use gin or spring water. When you pour libation always sit a few minutes to listen to what the Spirit is saying to you.

Akwasiadae is the most important sacred day for the Ancestors. Akwasiadae comes every 40-42 days and is always on a Sunday. One should prepare special foods on that day. Food and drink are very important in relationships particularly when visiting or being visited. It is a social gesture that always means welcome. Akan protocol dictates that when anyone visits our home we must offer them something to drink at the least. If food is cooked and available, we also offer them food. Thus, we feed our Ancestors whom we know live on a different plane, but who we believe should be offered the same sustenance that the living need. As protocol dictates, we are welcoming the Ancestors into our homes and our lives because they continue to be a part of family. They are responsible for protecting and guiding us and we are responsible for inviting them to share a meal with us.

The traditional ritual food for the Ancestors is called Eto. Following is the recipe for Eto.

Eto is prepared by using an African white yam. Peel and cook the yam until it is soft enough to mash. Mash the yam and divide into 2 batches. One batch will remain white and you can shape it into ball or egg shaped, your choice. You must add Palm oil or Red Oil to that 2nd batch. Mix well and shape into your favorite shape. Both balls can be placed on the same platter or separate platters, if you choose. Place peeled hard boiled eggs on the platter with the Eto. These eggs represent life. When you feed your Ancestors, you too must eat some of the Eto. This Eto is served every Akwasiadae and on other special days such as festivals, rites of passage or other celebrations.

Another way that you can feed your Ancestors is to cook your Ancestors' favorite meal and if you don't know what that is, cook your own favorite meal, and just make it special. This however is not in lieu of the Eto; it is in addition to the Eto. Then place water and drink on the altar and burn a candle. Sit and acknowledge that ancestor in a familiar way thanking them for guidance and all the things you believe that they have done for you. You will also want to do special things for your Ancestors on birthdays or other special family occasions. You can prepare food, place flowers in the vase, or fruit on the special plate or bowl on the altar. Just do something special!

It is up to you to establish a personal relationship and rapport with your Ancestors. This means spending time at your altar, placing food, fruit, and drink on the altar. Pouring libation periodically is also a good idea. Even though they know what is going on in your life, honor them by telling them what is happening, where you need help or guidance or just thanking them for the help that is being given.

There is no right or wrong way to pour libation for your Ancestors as long as it is done with great respect and reverence. Following is a simple procedure for libation. First you light the candle. Next, you pour drink into the small libation glass. Then ring the bell to summon your Ancestors. Then you start to pray calling God first, the rivers associated with you and your family next. After each body of water that you name, pour a small amount of drink into the bowl. Next call your family Ancestors and again after each name that you call, you must pour a small amount or drop of drink into the libation bowl. You say the word "Nsa" which means drink; or you can say, "have a drink" as you pour the drink into the bowl. After calling all, then you thank them for what you feel they have done for you. Next you petition them for whatever you need, if you need something. Finally, you will thank them in advance for what they are doing for you. You end the libation by pouring the last of the drink into the bowl and saying the word, "Yoooooooooo…," which is a common ending in Twi that means among other things, "the end."

An Akwasiadae Altar

The following is an example of an Ancestral Libation, which you may use until you are comfortable enough to add or change it. Before you call any of your Ancestors you must first honor God Almighty but do not offer a drink…just hold the glass. You offer the drink only from the name Asase Yaa (Mother Earth) and down.

An Ancestral Libation

Onyame, Almighty God, I call you because it is you alone who has established this system whereby I can be in close contact with my Ancestors. I acknowledge that in all things you have the ultimate power over everything that I do or ask. I know that you are with me, around me and have established your system of Ancestral Spirits for me. Thank you for my life, my health and my strength. I also thank you for my family.

Asase Yaa: Mother Earth, the one who provides sustenance for us everyday all day. I call you. *Nsa*

I call all the rivers and waters associated with me, my family, and my Ancestors:

Potomac River	Nsa
Ohio River	Nsa
Absecon River	Nsa
Volta River	Nsa
Mavis Bank River	Nsa

Now I wish to call all of my Ancestors.

Momma Helen	Nsa
Cousin Chris	Nsa
Auntie Tine	Nsa
Uncle Joe B.	Nsa

I call all of my Ancestors who I may not know who are willing to assist me in my journey on this earth.

Nsa

This is (your name) calling you to commune with me for a little while. First of all, thank you for all the doors that you have opened for me. Thanks for my new job with a raise. Thank you for giving me guidance in that situation I mentioned to you before. Thanks for helping the children in school...their grades are improving.... (Nsa)

I know that you continue to lookout for me. I am asking you just to help me have peace of mind in these situations and challenges that are before me. (Nsa) Help me to maintain order and understanding of my role in life.(Nsa) Help me to continue on my Spiritual path and to do those things to help me and my family to grow.(Nsa)

Nananom, I know that you will do this for me. And, I thank you for your assistance.
Yooooooooooooooo. (Pour out all of the drink)

Chapter 4

THE TRADITIONAL AKAN RELIGIOUS SERVICE

The Akan religious service called **Akom** is a participatory event. It is comprised of drumming, singing and dancing the ancient songs and rhythms of our Ancestors. These highly Spiritual ceremonies are lead by an Ordained Priest who holds the title of Okomfo Panyin and is recognized as the Senior Priest in the Shrine House. This Okomfo Panyin has undergone many years of specialized training to serve as intermediaries between the Deities and the people. The vigorous training includes instructions in the laws, taboos, ancient dances, ancient songs, and various idiosyncrasies of the Deities as well as general priestly duties. Thus, the Okomfo Panyin is able to handle the Spiritual energy that is created during an Akom service. During the course of the ceremony, other Akomfo (Priests and priestesses) allow certain Deities to possess them in order to give messages, guidance, perform healing, and encourage the people in attendance. The Akomfo take on the characteristics of the Deities when possessed and are able to dance, sing and relay messages from the Abosom. It is a highly Spirited event in which all attendees are invited to participate in the singing and dancing in order to fully benefit from the energy that is present.

Okomfowaa (Trainee) Dancing at An Akom in Ghana

The Akom

Our Ancestors are great! They had the wisdom to know that God is in everything and that we have the power and ability to experience God in many ways. The Traditional Akan religious service known as an Akom is a great example of our ability to experience the gifts from God. In Akan culture, you cannot separate the culture from the Spiritual element. As previously stated, the culture is steeped in tradition and in protocol. You will find various forms of protocol in every step of the Akom, which creates order to the event.

Preparation for an Akom sometimes begins very early in the day of the Akom. For special Akoms or festivals, preparation might begin several weeks ahead of the appointed time. Akoms are spiritual celebrations at which the Word of God comes directly through the Abosom who has possessed an Okomfo. It is an event that specifically invites God to appear through the Abosom using the trained Okomfo as the medium. The Akom is comprised of ancient drumming, singing and dancing as the Deities display their character using the Akomfo who is trained and have dedicated their lives to becoming a vehicle of the Abosom.

Appropriate Akom Attire

Those who are initiated to the Akan Akom Tradition typically wear traditional Akan clothes. Those who are not initiated to the traditional Akan Religion wear whatever is comfortable for them. Most people often wear clothes that they would normally wear to the religious order with which they are familiar recognizing that this is also a sacred space. Akomfo and Akomfowaa dress in a very specific manner. Traditional Akan attire is as follows:

Priests (male and female) dress in blue and white or all white for special occasions. Females wear lappas or wrappas, which is cloth wrapped in a traditional manner. This is worn with a matching blouse known as a Kabba. The mature women wear double (2) lappas; single women wear one lappa. For special celebrations, young girls can wear African cloth in a traditional manner, which is criss-crossed around the neck. Normally, women do not wear pants to an Akom. Of course, this would apply especially to those initiated to the Shrine House. Low heel shoes or traditional sandals are worn. When a woman is experiencing her menstrual cycle, it is customary to designate this by wearing a scarf or duku on her head. This informs Akomfo and those who are initiated to the Shrine House who may have blood taboos. Otherwise, the head may be covered or uncovered. Most often, the female Akomfo will wear a headwrap until their Deity is ready to possess them.

Male Akomfo wear knickers or shorts plus a traditional entoma; a batakari suit, or any other traditional outfit such as a political suit or fugu with slacks. This depends primarily on what their particular deity prefers. Male practitioners wear the same thing as described for the Akomfo except they may use different colors with the exception of funeral cloth. The designation of the Akomfo will be the ahenies, beads or other talisman or implements that the Akomfo will carry. These designations may not be apparent to the uninitiated. The Tegare and Nkwatia Kwatia systems' Akomfo have more choices than the White clothe Deities who are generally more particular and specific in their demands.

Female Akomfowaa wear white single lappas with shorts and tube tops underneath; while the male Akomfowaa wear white shorts and T-shirts or long white pants rolled up to the calf with a T-shirt. Again, wearing a duku will designate the females who are experiencing their menstrual cycle. This is done to inform any initiated person of the presence of flowing blood which some Deities do not entertain while others do not care. So this is a necessary courtesy for all in attendance.

Practitioners who are initiated to Akan Shrines wear blue and white or any other colors that are not funeral colors, unless they are in mourning. These clothes are worn in a normal, traditional manner the same as described for Akomfo.

The Akom Orchestra

Akoms typically start with a drum call by the sacred orchestra, which is comprised of various types of drums and bells. There are three (3) main drums used namely the Aprenting, Akorbor, and Aprede.

1. The **Aprenting** is a very low pitched drum that can be played with hands or sticks. It is used as the improvisation drum.

2. The **Akorbor** is the middle pitched drum, which is played with the hands.

3. The **Aprede** is the smallest drum and it has the highest pitch. This drum is played with long sticks.

There are other popular instruments used to enhance the sounds of the main drums. They are:

*   The **Donno** which is a double headed drum that is played with one hooked stick.

- The **Brekete**, a low pitched, double-headed drum is similar to the Donno, but larger. It can be played with the hand or the stick. It is recognized for its improvisations.

- The Dawaro or bells that are played with sticks accompany the drums.

- The **Mpomporo,** or clapping sticks, are played by the singers to accompany their singing with a steady beat that keeps the tone and the pace for the rest of the singing ensemble.

These Akom instruments are very special to the ceremony. They are sacred and usually have ancient Shrine medicine on the outside or inside. This medicine reinforces the energy and the power of the instruments. Specially initiated drummers are used to drum on the sacred drums that are used for the Akom. The drumming is not the same as drumming for African dance or other performances. There are special rhythms and some are specific to certain Deities. The drummers are specially trained and initiated to this service. However, other drummers may be used if the initiated drummers are unavailable.

The Spirit of God recognizes the drumming, these other instruments and sounds as an invitation to come into the presence of the gathering using the vehicles that have been established for the traditional religion, that is, the Abosom and sometimes the Nsamanfo. This Drum Call marks the official beginning of the Akom. All minds then become focused on what is about to happen. Practitioners open their hearts and minds in anticipation of the greater possibilities for that time. They participate in this order by clapping their hands or Mpomporo to the rhythm of the drums.

Entering the Sacred Space of the Akom

When the sacred space is created the attendees are encouraged to remove their shoes, socks, stockings, head ties, scarves, eyeglasses and any gold to prepare them for entering the consecrated boundaries of the sacred circle.

Once this occurs, the Chief Priest or Okomfo Panyin, arrives with other Akomfo and Akomfowaa to greet all participants moving from right to left using their right hand to shake the hands of attendees or to wave. Exceptions are when the females are experiencing menstrual cycles at which time they will simply use another form of acknowledgement without touching attendees. The other exception is that the Okomfo Panyin may choose not to touch people when greeting at a festival due to certain sensitivities of the occasion.

It is customary for the participants and visitors alike to return the greeting of the entourage. A member of the Shrine House will lead the attendees around the sacred circle for the customary greeting. These greetings are always proceed right to left regardless of who is in the room. The right hand is used to greet and the traditional Koto is used when appropriate. Women who are experiencing menstrual cycles will not touch or extend their hands to greet, rather they will use another form of acknowledgement, i.e. cross hands across chest, right hand into left hand, or simply raise the right hand in a slight wave. The same process is used for exiting the Akom.

When leaving the Akom, it is customary to request permission from the Okomfo Panyin. This is done by asking one of the primary Akom attendants to take the message of your pending departure to the Senior Okomfo. This is done so that travel blessings can be given for your safe journey. In the event that a spiritual message has been given for you, the Okomfo Panyin has an opportunity to relay the message to you prior to your departure. When leave is granted and the person or entourage is ready to exit, an attendant will again lead you around the sacred circle to say goodbye. When a Deity is present, the attendant will also inform the Deity of the request. Sometimes the Deity will opt to interact directly with the person; bestowing blessings or giving messages before the leave.

This is the customary protocol for Akoms.

Libation to Open the Akom

In order to open the Akom, the Okomfo Panyin appoints someone to pour libation, which is an ancient form of prayer to formally and verbally invite the Abosom and Nsamanfo to the Akom. Only on very special occasions does the Okomfo Panyin actually pour libation, as there are usually other Akomfo present who can perform that ritual.

The Okomfo pouring libation typically asks Nyame, the Abosom and Nsamanfo for blessings for the people who are gathered and who are enroute to the event. They pray for messages to be conveyed to those who are waiting, healing for those who need healing in any way, and to generally help those in need.

This particular Libation also creates a sacred space which, when possible, is marked by powder or white clay. This consecrates the boundaries for participants and Deities to enter for the special event. In Ghana this is always done. In the Diaspora, we are sometimes restricted by our venue to put powder or clay on the floor. However, the libation makes whatever space we occupy at that moment, a sacred space.

Akom Sacred Singers

Akom Singing—Energy of the Akom

The order of service continues with specific songs in an order that acknowledges all of the known Deities and those who are not presently known to us in the Diaspora. These ancient songs are all *Call and Response*, and are sung in a congregational style, in the language of Twi. The dialect of Twi depends upon which Deity we are trying to attract.

Some of the translations of the songs have been lost over the years. Additionally, in the Diaspora, we may or may not know all of the meanings of the songs due to the language barrier; however, we do know that they are praises for the wonderful work that Almighty God is doing through the Abosom and Nsamanfo. They also speak to the character, strength and work of the Deities. Even though the songs are sung in a different language, they are relatively easy to follow because they are sung in the *Call and Response* style, which we in the Diaspora are familiar.

The energy of the Akom lies primarily with the sacred singers. It is they who call the Deities down through their words of appellation and enthusiasm. So we sing them with as much vigor, enthusiasm and energy as we can muster up. When all the singers are engaged and totally immersed in their intent to appease the Deity, no one can sit very long in this inspirational atmosphere without tapping their feet or clapping their hands or moving in some other way. When the singers are dragging the songs or singing with their attention obviously focused on 'something else' then the Akom will lose momentum, eventhough the orchestra is playing so sweetly. This is cause for various forms of sanctions imposed on the sacred singers who are often comprised of Akomfo as well as anointed singers.

Attendees are encouraged to participate in the celebration by joining in the singing. It is not necessary to know the songs, but they are encouraged to try to follow the responses to the songs by listening and picking up the words in the way most of us are familiar. Likewise, attendees are encouraged to join in the dancing to the exciting ancient rhythms being played by the Akom orchestra. Those who are not initiated Akomfo or Akomfowaa are not expected to know the exact dance steps. Thus, anyone in attendance can dance freely as the Spirit moves with the steps that they know. Most often, this means follow the rhythm of the heartbeat. Participation in the singing and dancing ensures that attendees receive the sought after blessings and sometimes messages from the Deities.

An Akom might begin by singing a general song to invite all of the Deities followed by songs for specific Deities. Following are a sample of the songs that are sung during an Akom. These songs are written phonetically since the Twi spelling would not make sense to those who do not know the language. Each song starts out with a *Call by the Lead Singer,* to get the attention of the main singers and the attendees, afterwhich the song begins.

Call to Readiness for the Song

Call: Ah won yo!

Response: Yo!

Call: Ah won yo!

Response: Yo!

Call: Ah won yo!

Response: Yo!

The First Song

You will notice that the first song is calling all of the Deities. The loose translation is "Hey, you come" and then the specific name of a Deity "(Nana Asuo Gyebi) you come". This informs the Deities of not only their invitation to come but also that certain Akomfo are present to carry them. It is a very important song. Each Shrine House has its own 'first' song.

Eye Won Bro (eye-yeh' wun bro)

Chorus: Eye Won Bro

Lead: Nana Asuo Gyebi Won Bro

Chorus: Eye Won Bro

Lead: Nana Esi Won Bro

Chorus: Eye Won Bro

Lead: Tegare Won Bro

Chorus: Eye Won Bro

Lead: Adadi Kofi Won Bro

Chorus: Eye Won Bro

Lead: Nkwatia won Bro

Chorus: Eye Won Bro

Lead: Nsamanfo Won Bro

Chorus: Eye Won Bro

Repeat

Subsequent Songs

Usually the songs of the major Deity in the particular Shrine House are sung next. In AFSANI, Nana Asuo Gyebi songs are next, then Nana Esi Ketewaa, Adade Kofi, Nkwatia Kwatia, and Tegare. This sequence is repeated until the Deities begin to display which does not usually take a long time.

A Nana Asuo Gyebi Song

This is a praise song acknowledging that Nana Asuo Gybei is a great healer and that his medicine is good. And, we are calling for his medicine.

Aye me won Adurro (Ay' me won Drow)

Lead:	Aye me won adurro, Asuo Gyebi, Aye me won adurro.
Chorus:	Aye me won adurro Asuo Gyebi, Aye me won adurro
Lead:	Aye me won adurro eye aye Asuo Gyebi, Aye me won adurro
Chorus:	Aye me won adurro Asuo Gyebi, Aye me won adurro.

Repeat the whole sequence of phrases

A Nana Esi Ketewaa Song

All of Nana Esi's songs begin with a special appellation followed by the actual song. Nana Esi dances gracefully and not too fast. She is beautiful using her duku or scarves as she dances.

Part I

Lead:	Esi Esi Esi Esi
Chorus:	Mmmmmmmmm
Lead:	Esi oh Esi oh Esi
Chorus:	Mmmmmmmmmmm
Lead:	A qua Be yeh
Chorus:	Yooo Esi.

Part II

Call:	Ah Quay, miti miti mo.
Response:	Ah yeh ah Quay
Call:	*Nana Esi mo
Response:	Ah ye ah Quay
Call:	Miti miti mo
Response:	Ay ye ah Quay
Call:	Nana Esi mo
Response:	Ay ye ah Quay

Repeat from *

An Adadi Kofi Song

Adadi Kofi is a warrior messenger. He dances very fast and sharp so his songs are very fast. Many practitioners and visitors shy away from his dances because they are so fast and performed with great precision and power. One of the songs used to call Adadi Kofi follows. His songs also have a standard introduction.

Part I

Call: Paa		**Response:** Chee
Call: Paa		**Response:** Chee
Call: Paa		**Response:** Chee

Part II

**Lead:	Bro Bro, Adadi Bro bro bro Bro bro Adadi Bro. Adade Bro oh
Chorus:	Bro Bro Adadi Bro bro bro Bro bro Adadi Bro
Lead:	Adade Bro oh
Chorus:	Bro bro Adadi Bro bro bro Bro bro Adade Bro

Repeat from ** using the following lead ad libs:

Lead ad Libs:	Adade Kofi Bro Bro Adade Bro

A Tegare Song

As previously stated, Tegare is a system of Deities. The songs sung for Nana Tegare are for all of the Deities in that system. Those Akomfo who are a part of the system know all the songs and dance to all the songs. One of the most important songs is the one that some Tegare Akomfo call their national anthem. It is calling Tegare using his most popular name as well as some of his aliases and asking him to come quick.

Part I

Lead:	Osi eye aye
	Bibi bo si eye aye
	Gari Akontihene osi eye aye
Chorus:	Osi eye aye
	Bibi bo si eye aye
	Gari, Akontihene osi eye aye
	Repeat

Part II

Lead:	Osi eye aye eye aye
	Gari be nine noo
Chorus:	Osi eye aye
Lead:	Tegare Be nine noo
Chorus:	Osi eye aye

Repeat sequence many times with the following Lead ad libs.

Aja be nine no
Baffour be nine no
Osi eye aye
Osi eye aye eye aye

Nana Tegare Listening To His "National Anthem"

A Song calling Mmoetia (Dwarfs)

As previously stated, Mmoetia is a system of Dwarfs. Within that system is Nkwatia Kwatia which is one of the most popular subsystems within the system. There are other Mmoetia throughout Ghana and the Diaspora. This song is one of the songs used to call them. The loose translation is: "Hey Mmoetia, I miss you. Where are you? Come and assist me. Show yourself." Mmoetia finally says, "I am here. I have come."

Aye Eye Mmoetia

Part I

Lead:	Aye a Tia, Aye A Tia, Mif me quio mo Nana bre me ni oh Aye a tia, aye a mmoetia, mif me quio mo Nana bre me ni oh.
Chorus:	Aye a Ti a, Aye a Ti a Mif me quio mo Nana Bre me ni oh

Repeat sequence many times.

Part II

Lead:	Aye a Ti a, Aye a Ti A Mif me quio mo Nana Bre me ni oh.
Call:	Aye ah Mmoetia!
Response:	Mmoetia ma bo!
Call:	Aye a Mmoetia
Response:	Mmoetia ma bo
Call:	Aye a Mmoetia
Response:	Mmoetia ma bo

Continue for some time then go back to the Verse. Repeat the whole sequence as many times as desired.

Mmoetia Turning

During Akoms, most frequently, the entire series of songs for each of the Deities are not sung because ultimately one of the Deities will possess an Okomfo and the 'real' Akom begins. Thus, another format becomes the priority and, that is, the songs of the displaying Deity are sung. The welcoming song, which each Deity has, and then other songs of appellation and praises are sung. Some songs are actually proverbs about the Deity's works and powers. There is much dancing at this time by the Deity who may subsequently ask attendees to join in the dance. Perhaps, a person who has been blessed by the Deity or has interacted with the Deity wants to give praise and honor for the work done. In that case, the person may elect to get up and dance without an invitation, which is welcomed. Other Deities may or may not appear however, at some point during the Akom, the songs for other Deities are sung to again give them an invitation to display as well as to acknowledge their work. When another Deity does appear, their songs are also incorporated in the repertoire of songs. All of the songs are praises, appellations, proverbs or thanksgiving.

Entering the Sacred Space to Dance

There is an established protocol for entering the sacred space of the Akom sacred circle to dance. When a person is compelled to enter the sacred boundaries to dance, they proceed right to left around the circle greeting people as they move towards the drum. When arriving in front of the Akom Orchestra, the dancer must salute the lead drum by kneeling in front of the lead drum and touching the floor with the knee and right hand 3 times. A slight Koto to the other sacred drums and instruments is also expected. This is to acknowledge the sacredness of the orchestra's role in summoning and playing for the Deities and also playing for the person dancing.

The dance is always counter clockwise. So the participant will begin dancing in that direction and continue saluting the whole circle to announce their intention to dance. This is done by placing the right hand into the left hand and bending a little as you are dancing in a stance to seek permission from those in charge and to acknowledge the presence of everyone in the circle. Then the dance is on.

The dance is ended in the same way by saluting the lead drum and orchestra as well as the members in the circle. You are actually showing thanks for supporting your participation in this experience as you added your energy to this Holy event. Uninitiated participants are not expected to dance with the same precision and skill as the long term members and initiated Akomfo who have been trained to perform the special dances of the Abosom. However, participants are expected to get up and dance with sincere anticipation of blessings from the Abosom.

Display of the Deities: Okomfo Spiritual Possession

The Akom has a serious and intense amount of Spiritual energy flowing. The drums, songs and initial dances invite the energy and appearance of the Deities. Most of the time, they do not disappoint us. The Akomfo who attend the Akom come with expectations that their particular Deity may decide to appear to bring blessings and messages to the attendees.

During an Akom, the Okomfo may spiritually possess their Deity. That is, the Bosom literally takes possession of the body and the mind of the Okomfo. Thus, a great transformation takes place in the persona of the individual as they release themselves to the power of the Deity. The individual is no longer in control of the dancing, singing and messages that might be presented. White powder or clay is applied upon the face and other parts of the body of the Okomfo to signify that they are in a *state of spiritual possession* and, in a sacred and holy state. Attendants dress the Bosom in his or her particular clothes and style. The Bosom is given particular implements and ahenies. The Bosom uses the Okomfo's body to dance their own dance, to sing their songs and to otherwise display themselves as they bring blessings to participants. **Nana Yao Opare Dinizulu always reminded the Okomfo: *"Possession is your Profession."*** So it is very important for Okomfo to be prepared to experience Spiritual possession on a regular basis. Sometimes, an Abosom will briefly possess an uninitiated person to heal, to encourage, or to strengthen them. Through this contact the Abosom will make himself known to the person.

Possession and display of a Deity is a very important part of the Akom in that the Abosom comes from the spiritual plane to use the Okomfo as a means of communicating on this earth plane with the people. It is a phenomenon that is not easy to understand intellectually, but is easier to assimilate within a Spiritual frame of reference.

In Ghana, I have seen many wonderful miracles as the Abosom use their power in the midst of people to help increase the faith of those present to the possibilities of healing mind, body and Spirit by the Deity. I have seen a person's leg healed on the spot as the deity removed nails out of the person's leg without cutting it. I have seen Deities take one leap and land in a tree or on a rooftop to display their powers. I have seen a certain deity jump into the sacred fire, not once but 3 to 4 times, and come out of the fire dancing and singing showing the power within. I have seen a Deity jump into a river and go under the water and stay for many minutes only to come up with messages for certain people. I have seen Deities use sharp knives cutting themselves or stabbing themselves, and never bleeding or penetrating the skin. Deities often spin or turn in a circle for very long periods of time and never fall or trip which shows the strength of the Deity.

All of this is done to impress upon the people the spiritual power inherent in the Abosom. When the possession is completed and the Deity leaves, the Okomfo returns to a normal state and may not remember any of the messages, dances or songs that were performed by the Deity. The Okomfo uses a lot of energy and usually is tired when all is completed. Therefore, most of the time, you will see the Okomfo who was previously in a state of possession, trying to relax a little.

In a village of the Eastern Region, a certain young woman whose mother was an Okomfo continuously doubted the power of the Abosom. She had even convinced her mother to attend church and renounce her profession as an Okomfo. Despite pleadings from other Akomfo, Osofo, Bosomfo and other believers, the former Okomfo did just that. She dropped her profession. Subsequently, that person's Deity came with a message from Nana Panyin, that if she did not continue in her profession she would become seriously ill and make her transition within a certain period of time. As foretold, this Okomfo became seriously ill and within the stated time period made her transition.

During her mother's illness, this young woman came to the Shrine begging for her mother. However, Nana Panyin had given the conditions which were unalterable. When the mother made her transition, and prior to the funeral, that certain young woman possessed her mother's Deity and stayed in a state of possession for several days non-stop. Finally, a senior Okomfo poured libation to ask for the return of the young woman so that funeral arrangements could continue for her mother, the deceased Okomfo. Since that time, this same young woman has been experiencing possession by her late mother's Deity and is known to remain in a state of possession for 2 to 3 days at a time. However, as of this writing, she has not committed to training, but has asked that rituals be performed so that she will not be required to take up the profession of Okomfo because her husband does not want it.

As of today, no one has agreed to perform the rituals because they remember her attempts to negate the power of this ancient Spiritual system. By the way, she no longer attends church and her former pastor gave up his profession. Though he is not a public participant in the ancient tradition and rituals of Akom, he does rely on the Shrines for spiritual assistance.

Possession is a thrilling phenomena and experience to witness! It also is a time for attendees to open themselves to the possibility of receiving whatever you need! I encourage each person who attends an Akom to get up and dance when you are given the opportunity.

Timing

In the Diaspora, the Akom typically continues for 2 to 3 hours. However, because it is so upbeat and spirited, the time usually passes rather quickly. Various Deities visit during this celebration. The Akom usually ends when all of the Deities have left. In some instances, the Deities who appear late in the Akom are asked to take leave. However, I have not seen this happen very often in Ghana, especially for the personal convenience of someone. I have seen it happen when it was out of concern for the Okomfo who is possessed. Perhaps the Okomfo has health issues and the Deity is being unduly rough, or some other major concern about the Okomfo. This is a human response that is often questioned by attending Akomfo and believers.

Some Deities are known to stay a very long time, sometimes for several days. I have even seen Deities travel back to the hometown on the van or car with the people who brought the Okomfo who is possessed. It is never an issue. In fact, it seems to be taken as a blessing and another miracle event.

Frequently, some type of refreshments or feast follows the Akom. As we know, traditional Akans take every opportunity to socialize and share a meal. During festivals, food is always served. The Akan Akom Tradition practitioners and well wishers must consume the sacrificial meat.

Akom Taboos

There are many taboos or otherwise inappropriate behaviors that have been established for Akoms, all of which are almost impossible to list. However, a few major taboos are as follows.

1. Do not greet anyone with your left hand. Having said that, there are two known Deities that do not mind a left-hand greeting. In fact, they both expect a left-handed greeting. They are Nana Panyin who is left-handed and Nana Tegare (and some members of the Tegare system) who may use either hand, but most likely the left-hand.

2. Do not gesture with your left hand, which is reserved for toilet use. This extends not only for Akoms but all the time. **An Akan Proverb states: *"One would not point to their home with their left hand."*** It is the same as cursing the home.

3. Do not enter the sacred circle during menstrual cycle unless specifically invited by a Deity such as Nana Tegare. Nana Panyin would not invite anyone cycled into the sacred circle.

4. Do not place your hands on top of your head during an Akom. This denotes that you are mourning the dead, which is inappropriate for the space designated for the living that understands the process of reincarnation. Therefore, one would have no reason to mourn when the event is set for honoring and celebrating transitions. Also, the Deities do not like crying which is usually accompanied with the hands on top of the head.

5. Do not enter the sacred circle with shoes and socks on your feet. The exception are Royals and Okomfo Panyin who are wearing traditional sandals and are required to keep sandals on their feet.

6. Do not enter the sacred circle when menstruating.

7. Do not assume that the Okomfo Panyin will shake your hand. Only extend your hand if that person extends their hand to you.

8. Do not take the lead in a dance when the Deity is dancing. You must dance behind the Deity.

9. The Okomfo Panyin or Senior Okomfo is guiding the energy of the Akom. Do not try to change that order.

10. Do not in any way offend the Okomfo Panyin or the Deity by bad behavior, such as not greeting, leaving without requesting permission, not acknowledging as you enter the circle to dance or some other outward display of disrespect.

11. Refusing to dance once you have been asked by a Deity or a Senior Okomfo who is guiding the Akom is an outward form of disrespecting authority and may result in you missing your blessing.

Chapter 5

Akomfo (Priests/Priestesses) and Other Ordained Spiritual Leaders in the Akan Akom Tradition

We have mentioned the importance of the Akomfo at the actual religious service. However, their role in the community at large is much broader. The Okomfo (Akomfo pl.) is the keeper of the Ancient Akan Akom Tradition which includes customs, protocol, historical religious and community rituals and ceremonies as well as knowledge about community personalities and events. Thus, this profession is coveted yet feared by most because of the importance of the position to the family and community, and the intense training that is required for the position.

The Akomfo belong to a sacred Spiritual order of dedicated men and women who are trained in the Spiritual tenets and customs of our Ancestors. Their primary job is to serve the Deities and the community. They serve the Deities by following their guidance and heeding their taboos. In addition to receiving training about the various Deities, Akomfo receive training in divination, traditional healing techniques, herbal medicine, rituals and ceremonies, customs and protocols. Though trained in many disciplines, the ultimate power comes from Almighty God and the Deities, especially in the delivery of messages, discerning Spirits and many other mystical powers used in their profession. They serve the community by providing the connection between God, the Abosom and the Ancestors. Akomfo have various skills and life experiences that complement their spiritual training. Akomfo are quite instrumental in the growth and development of the community at large.

In Ghana, full recognition and understanding of the position is gathered though observation, experience, oral accounts and a lifetime of personal contact. Thus there is a basis for the Godly fear. In the Diaspora, the person who heeds the call is doing so from an ancestral remembering experience where the family ancestor is calling a family member to take up the profession that previously has been a part of that family. It is not an easy decision to turn from all the uninformed teaching and preaching against African religion that we in the Diaspora have endured for many years. The open heart of the seeker comes into play and accepts the Call based on strong faith that this is our ancestral inheritance. The belief that just as Almighty God has sanctioned other religious orders, He too has created this call to *Sankofa*. This is much stronger than any of the attempted mental manipulations from family, church, educational institutions and other mechanisms that we have experienced.

Often times, the person who is "called" to the profession tells stories about their path to becoming an Okomfo. One person recounted that he had dreams and out of body experiences in which his Ancestors confronted him about his responsibility to the clan. Another person says all of her life has been dedicated to some spiritual calling. Howevershe was never satisfied with her position because it did not involve cultural identity. Others maintain that they have been official seekers, meaning they have tested many religions and found something lacking, and primarily cultural identification. There are numerous stories about this particular soul journey.

Often in these days of high tech and surfing the Internet, some initiates have admitted to browsing many websites on African religion. However, a particular one resonated with them, which captured their curiosity or stirred up their ancestral calling which subsequently led them to initiation. Even some have even been initiated into another system that is not Akan, only to decide later that Akan resonates more with their ancestral family wishes and vice versa. The quest for a deep spiritual transformation is the common thread whether the person immediately realizes it or not.

One thing that is also common among seekers is that most do not initially understand all that is involved in the intitation and practice process. Some seekers might see the glamour in the rituals, the dress, the comportment, the attention, and the privileges that the Akomfo receive. However, what they don't see is the very stringent and challenging requirements and discipline associated with Okomfo training. During training every personal belief, characteristic, behavior, perspective, norm and habit are challenged. Some very difficult decisions relative to family upbringing including beliefs, superstitions, attitudes, acquired mannerisms, and normal operatives are required, as we become more involved in becoming an Okomfo. The initiate begins to realize that they can no longer operate in a private vacuum, because their lives become open to community scrutiny. Akomfo are expected to become respected community leaders and role models as well as spiritual mediums.

The training process on becoming an Okomfo is quite arduous, rigorous and lengthy. We always warn the initiate that this is a lifetime commitment to learning and practicing the culture. Some of this falls on deaf ears because the greater attraction is about having the same power as is sometimes displayed by the Deities, the glamour associated with being an Okomfo, and the status that one gets post graduation. Many believe that they can withstand the rigors of training in order to gain any one or all of the potential outcomes. However, many start and many fall by the wayside. Some resume their training at a later date as they realize that once one has started on this ancestral path and touched by the Abosom, it is very difficult to walk away.

Information about the Akan initiation processes, as well as many other religious initiations, is given on a need to know basis. It is not for public information to appease the curiosity seekers. However, general discussion follows which outlines those aspects that can be shared.

The intense journey of the Okomfo begins when he or she identifies the Shrine house of their choice, which is the physical repository of the religious practices, principles, medicines and vessels. This happens after the call, which may or may not begin with an actual physical introduction to an event. Often the proposed initiate attends some type of event that introduces him or her to the Akan culture. This is usually by invitation from a practitioner many months prior to the actual visit. It is not uncommon to have many interruptions in the flow of an invitation to an Akan event to the actual attendance to an event. But somehow, the Ancestors will expose the proposed initiate at the appropriate time and place. Typically, the seeker attends more than one event and consequently experiences some type of personal connection to the culture, which may be superfluous, or of a deeper spiritual connection. Ultimately, the person might seek information from a practitioner, most times not even a priest, who will lead the way. Thus, the journey begins.

After becoming a member of a Shrine house by constant participation or divination, the person is led to initiation as an Okomfowaa, or priest in training. This process varies from organization to organization but all have a period of seclusion to initiate the person to their specific deity which is acknowledged during the process. At that time, the new initiate is given a shrine name which he or she will carry the rest of their lives. Certain initiation rituals are performed during the period of seclusion and consistently during the training period. The formal training period varies by individuals but is usually at least 3 years and sometimes more. It depends on the performance and commitment of the Okomfowaa. The identifying factor among Okomfowaa is the hair, which is worn in Mpesi mpesi, which is a very unique style that is often mistaken for the popular style called dreadlocks. However, there is a big difference in that it is specially treated and is the vehicle, which helps to facilitate communication between the Okomfowaa and the Abosom. At the end of the training, the Okomfowaa's hair is cut, except in very special cases which are dictated by the Abosom.

MPESI PESI

During training the Okomfowaa travels a very intense individual spiritual journey in preparation for this profession. The new Okomfowaa is charged with learning the character, songs, dances and loads of information about their personal Deity as well as other known Dieities. Other pertinent information such as family and community rituals, medicines, and protocols are taught. They become the repositories of Akan history, community knowledge and traditions, customs and taboos that are revealed during this period of time. Most of the information is privileged information and shared only on a need to know basis, and perhaps not on the same level as all other Akomfo. Every Okomfo has the opportunity to acquire the knowledge of traditional medicine use of herbs, roots and other items that nature provides. They can become an herbalist, though an herbalist, or Densini as known in the Twi language, is not necessarily a priest. The extent to which an Okomfowaa receives information is driven by that person's own initiative to memorize, internalize, practice and display an understanding of the trusted information. Again, the depth of the information shared by an Okomfo

Panyin with the trainee is usually dependent on the loyalty, trust, and proven character of the individual.

Though stated very succinctly, the training period is a time of personal transformation for each initiate. Some experience this transformation quite easily and submissively; others refuse to surrender to the lessons that the Abosom and Nsamanfo are trying to convey to them. There is a partnership in the training process between the trainee, Okomfo Panyin, the Abosom and Nsamanfo. The training period is a time of spiritual transformation for each initiate. It is very personal and is almost always experienced quite differently from person to person. The level of difficulty in maintaining the cultural and spiritual taboos is dependent upon the individual's commitment. Even though each year of training is experienced differently by each person, a certain level of proficiency must be reached before a person is ready for graduation, which is the beginning of another phase.

As the preparation for graduation approaches, the Okomfowaa experience a greater amount of pressure to succeed in retaining information, knowing all of the characteristics of their patron Deity and knowing how to display their Deity including possession, dancing, and singing the songs of the Deity. This period is marked by much strain on the psyche of the trainee in anticipation of the final testing and presentation to the community. Additionally, the Okomfowaa is aware that the full direction and protection of the Okomfo Panyin lessens. Thus, the new Okomfo must be ready to stand on their own.

A clear example of this independence is similar to the growth and development of a child. First, the Mother becomes pregnant, carries the baby, delivers the baby, teaches and nurtures the baby and at 18 years of age the child is now grown and ready to venture on its own receiving limited direction. This limited direction is sometimes initiated by the child who declares independence and a "know it already" attitude, versus the one who knows that they need further direction and does not stray too far from Mother until they are absolutely sure they are on the right track. Even then, the new Okomfo sticks fairly close to the wisdom and guidance that they have enjoyed…and can be counted on to continue the relationship with the Mother.

So it is Spiritually with the Okomfo Panyin and Okomfowaa/Okomfo. Relationship. Many times, this relationship is interrupted because of the empty nest syndrome; not wanting to sever the natal cord, as in child rearing; teaching and learning fatigue; and misunderstanding regarding roles and responsibilities. The student is now led to another teacher to further their studies in a specific area that may not be available from their Godmother. It is then that a Godmother may feel somehow threatened or betrayed if there has not been a student/teacher discussion and understanding. Other reasons exist such as family pressure or interference, relocation, child rearing, and for other more personal reasons. Whatever the case, there is always a Spiritual connection between the Godmother (Okomfo Panyin) and the student (new Okomfo) whether physically or openly acknowledged, or not. Of course, for the sake of an example for the upcoming Okomfowaa, it is always preferred that the relationship continues in an honest and open manner. One of the responsibilities of an Okomfo is to maintain the culture, protocols and information learned during training. Ultimately, it is incumbent upon the new Okomfo to continue studying every aspect of being an Okomfo. This is considered to be the same as graduate and postgraduate studies and just as the natural mother is proud of this accomplishment, so it is with the Spiritual mother or Godmother.

The Late Nana Serwaa of Ejisu with Okomfowaa

Each Okomfo is different and has a different calling. There are many shrine positions that require the assistance of a graduate Okomfo. Thus, after graduation, an Okomfo may or may not be required to establish his or her own station immediately, and may or may not be called to establish their own Shrine house. However, each Okomfo is expected to pour libation, maintain the tenets of the Akan Akom Tradition, and maintain the implements of their Deity. Some new (and older) Okomfo continue to serve the parent shrine and Okomfo Panyin for the rest of their lives. In Ghana, it is expected that the new Okomfo serve in that capacity for at least 3 years before establishing any type of independent Shrine house. There is much work to do at the parent shrine that only a graduate Okomfo can perform such as rituals, the upkeep of the implements and Shrines, assisting in the actual work with clients, initiations, helping to teach new Okomfowaa songs, dances, protocol, history and much more. The longer and more consistent a new Okomfo serves the Godmother, the more that person will learn about the Shrines. It is during this time that they will receive privileged information about Akom. Thus, this requirement benefits all involved and also ensures better-qualified Okomfo.

Every Okomfo has a station at their place of residence. No Okomfo wants to be far from their shrine and implements. This station is where they can do personal and family consultations and other limited Spiritual work mostly with family as well as a select group of other clients. However, the Okomfo may be assigned to a station in another location to satisfy the needs of that community and the Parent Shrine. For example, each town has a patron Deity that protects the town. Typically, there is an Okomfo who is responsible for the upkeep of the Shrine and usually is the one who possesses that Deity giving messages to the Chief as required.

**The Late Nana Ama Odi
Dempti Komfo Panyin of Mampong Akwapim**

Establishing a Shrine house is a much more challenging situation in that the Okomfo is establishing an organization. This organization is open to membership and presents opportunities for Spiritual training and teaching in the traditional Akan methods. This places an enormous responsibility on the Okomfo. This is actually where they can invite others to join and become a part of an organization. Training other priests and shrine members is the norm here.

Another important position that requires an enormous amount of training is that of the **Bosomfo** who are owners of Shrines. They may have one or more Deities that they are taking responsibility for keeping in conjunction with an Okomfo, or alone. Some Bosomfo actually possess this Deity but more often than not the Bosomfo does not possess or carry the Deity. They receive a similar training as the Okomfo but the focus is not on possession or displaying the deity. Their focus is on all of the rituals and associated duties. The Bosomfo is the historian of the shrine house, knows when and how the rituals are to be performed and know the hierarchy of the positions. The Bosomfo is responsible for the replacement of an Okomfo Panyin if one has not been appointed prior to their departure.

Another scenario identifies the Bosomfo as one who may be working solo having inherited Shrines because they somehow took an oath to take care of the shrine. In this case, the person is required to undergo training in order to know what is expected. That person must have a teacher which is usually sent through divine intervention. The Bosomfo also may have been called by a Deity to that position. Sometimes, it is mistaken for a call to become an Okomfo, however it becomes apparent that this is not the case since the person never possess the Deity even though they learn all the songs, dances, rhythms, characteristics and other nuances.

The Bosomfo does not train and cannot ordain Akomfo but an Okomfo can train and ordain a Bosomfo. Nevertheless, it is a coveted position and held in very high esteem because this person is the holder of very important information which is their primary focus.

Another important Spiritual position is that of a **Densini** or herbalist. The Mmemotia who are keepers of the knowledge about all leaves, plants and traditional medicine calls this highly trained person to the position. The Densini is not an Okomfo and may or may not possess a Deity. However, all have Deities, which are most likely Dwarfs, who work with them and inform them of various traditional medicine and cures. The Densini has the same level of training as the Okomfo, however their focus is primarily on herbs and their relationship to the healing aspect of the ancient Akan religion. These Denisini are sought out by Okomfo many times to get medicine for specific cases. It is a known fact that the Okomfo's Deity might actually send that person to a Densini to retrieve the medicine. The Densini spends an enormous amount of time with nature, in the woods or other natural surroundings and sanctuaries. They too must learn the dances of the Deities especially the Dwarfs.

Each Okomfo has a **Shrine Okyeame.** This is the person who has been trained in all aspects of the operations of the Shrine. The Okyeame knows the behavior, the food, drink, dress, dance, drumming and songs of the Deity or Deities that their Okomfo Panyin is serving. When the Okomfo possesses their Deity, it is the duty of the Shrine Okyeame to serve as the intermediary in communicating messages between the Deity and the attendees. The Okyeame is also the formal messenger for the Okomfo Panyin. When sent with a message, it is the same as the Okomfo Panyin speaking. Therefore, they must be articulate, know proverbs and be spiritually astute. The Okyeame undergoes formal as well as apprentice training for many years and receives the protection of the Shrine in many ways. He or she is also responsible for knowing the history of the Shrine House and the Okomfo. The Shrine Okyeame is a very important and coveted position and not to be taken lightly. The responsibilities are great in the function of the Shrine and the Okomfo. The Okyeame is sometimes awarded certain powers for services to the Deities and Okomfo.

Another very important position in the Shrine House is the **Obrafo**. In addition to knowing the work of the Okyeame, this assistant is trusted to do much of the work of maintaining the Shrines. It is the Obrafo who is instrumental in the proper preparation and execution of the rituals when presenting life force offerings to the Deities. The Obrafo must know the food and drink of the Deities; the likes and dislikes of the Deities; and the proper manner to feed the Deities. They are the keepers of information regarding the conduct of necessary rituals for most situations in the Shrine. The Obrafo has the ear of the Okomfo and protects the Okomfo at all costs. The Obrafo is highly skilled and trained in the ancient ways of the Shrines and Deities. They are to be feared for their knowledge and skill in maintaining order. They are usually the somewhat quiet but, make no mistake about it, they are the natural warriors of the Shrine house. When an Obrafo speaks, they are taken very seriously.

Additionally, there are very skilled persons who are always visible in an invisible posture around the Shrine Houses known as the **Bosomkorafo**. They are involved in the intricacies of maintaining the Shrine House's overall appearance. They are the informal messengers and often run special errands for the Okomfo because they know the important people for their particular Shrine. They are usually found living in the Shrine compound or are around the Shrine house at all times. The Bosomkorafo are very close to the Okomfo Panyin. They are trusted in private places around the Shrine House where many people are not allowed to enter. These assistants know the history of the Shrine, the nuances of the Okomfo, and are able to perform any of the jobs necessary to the smooth function of the Shrine. Most are not Okomfo and do not possess a specific Deity. However, they may know the songs and dances of all the Deities associated with their Shrine House. And, similar to other Shrine assistants, these Bosomkorafo may have personal Shrines given to them for their unwavering dedication and loyalty to the Shrines and Okomfo Panyin.

Another coveted position in the Shrine House is the **Akom Gyegyefo**. This person is most visible when the Akom is being performed. He or she is responsible for serving the Deity. This is the person who dresses the Deity when the Okomfo possesses. The Akom Gyegyefo carries the towel, powder or clay, and the Florida Water around with the Deity. This assistant stays very close to the Deity and is always ready if the Deity needs something. He or she makes certain that the Deity's appearance is in proper order including the clothes and implements. For example, Nana Asuo Gyebi and Nana Esi Ketewaa are quite particular about their appearance. The Gyegyefo must know this fact and others about all the Deities the Okomfo Panyin serves. Further, this person maintains the clothes and towels of the Deity which includes washing, ironing, folding and doing what ever is necessary to have them ready when the Okomfo possesses the Deity. A major responsibility of the Akom Gyegyefo is to make sure that the Deity does not fall and that there is nothing in the space that would block the Deity's dance or performance of their work. This is also a coveted and trusted position due to the close proximity of the person to the Deity. The Akom Gyegyefo must be a highly spiritual person who has been trained specifically to know all aspects of the Deity's display, characteristics, attire and many other nuances.

All of the foregoing positions are ordained positions. Eventhough the ordination process are not the same, there are some commonalties. The most impressive one is that each person must be trained and highly skilled in his or her position. The training never ends. Secondly, each person must maintain high standards and follow the protocols and beliefs of the Akan Akom Tradition. They are all considered to be spiritual leaders and another repository of very important and privileged information. Often, they are seen with at least one apprentice helping them perform their duties. It is not easy for one to step into these positions unless there is an obvious call by a Deity.

Ordination and Graduation consists of many rituals and ceremonies. Parts of the ordination and graduation rituals are performed secretly, however there may be some public displays. In the case of the Okomfo there usually is a public display of spirit possession including singing and dancing. Family, friends and others, who are interested, usually attend the public display. After which, the newly ordained Spiritual leader is sometimes placed in seclusion for an additional period of time in order to receive proprietary information only entrusted with a graduate and to undergo certain specific secret rituals specific to their position.

After a required number of years of formal training and the necessary post graduate studies, Akomfo, Abosomfo, and Densini, are able to establish their own work stations known as Shrine houses. After all of these processes, these ordained spiritual leaders are qualified, in varying degrees depending on the individual's commitment to learning and knowing, to emerge and represent themselves as an Okomfo, Bosomfo, or Densini. Time seasons the Spiritual Leader and again it is up to each individual to continue learning a lifetime of information at their own pace. The Okomfo holds all privileges and is able to perform all rituals on a limited basis pertaining to life and death. Some rituals are reserved for the more seasoned Okomfo, Bosomfo or Elder, and in some instances, women who have passed menses.

The community has indeed received a gift when a new Okomfo or other traditional Spiritual leader emerges, as that signifies another connection to our Ancestors and the ancient ways of our Ancestors. This connection further ensures that the indigenous Akan culture and religion will never die or be eradicated.

Chapter 6

PROCEDURES FOR CLEARING OFFENSES AGAINST DEITIES, AKOMFO, ROYALS, ELDERS, SHRINE HOUSE

The ancient Elders say: *"Tradition remains in the ear."*

Intentional disrespect for an Akan person whether they are from the Royal family, an Okomfo, or layperson, in the Akan culture, results in a requirement to apologize. This act of defiance is taken very seriously because it reflects a total disregard for a traditional code of conduct which has been established by our ancient Ancestors. No matter what your opinion of the person may be, their position must always be recognized and respected. In addition to reverence and respect, the positions of Royals and Akomfo are sacred. Disrespect of God's anointed and ordained as well as the Ancestor's anointed translates to disrespect for the entire Akan cultural system. An offense is not only to the person but also to the sanctity of the stool, which represents the community and the continuity of their clan. The Royals are links to the ancestral world and those of us living on earth. If you witness or are aware of the sacred spiritual rituals performed for Royals and Akomfo at their enstoolment, you know without a doubt that the positions are sacred. An offense to the sacred stool and person who occupies the stool causes an imbalance and unharmonious effect in the community. Therefore, these offenses require sacred spiritual rituals to bring the community back into balance. These rituals have already been established by our Ancestors and continue to be conducted as prescribed. It must be recognized that these ancient procedures maintain peace, harmony and balance in the community and family, which extends beyond the one person to whom the offense was committed.

It must be noted that even though these positions are grouped together, there is a hierarchy within the positions. The Royals (Chiefs, Queenmothers) are first in the hierarchy and placed according to the status of their stools and tenure of the person on the stool. They are the custodians of the Clan stools and the Ancestors. The Akomfo, Elders, Shrine house and other royal courtiers all have an order within their grouping. Once these apologies have been performed and accepted the incident is off limits for future discussion. The slate is clean and it should be business as usual. The protocol for the apology is as follows.

The offended person cannot and should not be approached directly, as they might not be ready to face the offender. Thus, an emissary must be designated to speak on the behalf of the offender to the offended's representative who is usually the Okyeame or Obrafo. This person approaches the primary representative of the offended to acknowledge the offense and to express the desire to apologize. That person will agree on a time, date, and location of the formal apology. There is no informal apology because all offenses are considered to be against the stool and Spirit of their Ancestors as well as the person who occupies the stool.

The items required for the apology have been established by the ancestors of the abusua (family) stool. These are articulated and negotiated to the extent that they can be negotiated. The determination is not made by the offender as to what will and will not be done. This is a negotiated agreement within the framework of the offended's stool requirements. For example, a stool might require one or more animal life force offering's (i.e. sheep, goat, chicken, dove, etc.); a drink such as gin, scotch, wine, or mineral water; traditional food such as eggs, yam, red oil for Eto, or other foodstuffs; money in a designated denomination such as 50,000 cedis, $1 or more; and a requirement to apologize in public. There may or may not be an opportunity to negotiate, however the final decision rests with the offended and the stool's primary requirements. These vary by stool and are known by the incumbent the Abusua Panyin and the elder family members. Therefore, though the requirements may appear to be severe, it is most likely commensurate with the offense. The main thing to remember is that it is up to the offended to accept or reject any offers for negotiation within the framework of the ancestors' wishes.

Many times I have experienced sitting on Council when an emissary is present to set up an apology. One recent experience involved a man who ignored a warning from the Chief not to build a certain extension to his house because it would interfere with sacred processions through the village. These processions could be funerals, enstoolments, or other events to honor the Ancestors. The man, who was not a family member but who was allowed to settle in the village, built the extension anyway after a direct discussion with the Chief and subsequently with the Elders. Even though he understood the Spiritual implications for the reason not to build, he considered the initial ruling unreasonable. His father an elderly man who should not have had to worry about such things was dispatched to beg an apology for him and to negotiate the fine. The final outcome was that the man had to apologize to the Chief because the ground upon, which he built, was on sacred ground, the Ancestors path for sacred ceremonies. The fine was reduced by one half of the initial demand out of respect for the old man designated as his emissary. The old man promised to personally have the structure removed. The offender then had to come forward with his emissary, who actually spoke the apology and presented the fine of 1 sheep instead of 2 sheep, 250,000 cedis instead of 500,000 cedis, 2 chickens instead of 3 chickens, and 3 bags of cement instead of 5 bags of cement, towards the village's development project.

Another recent example, is the case of an Okomfo who attended a festival but did not bring a possession bag, as is required of an Okomfo. Of course, his Deity came and demanded sacred display items. This was an unfortunate situation that involved everyone from the Shrine including other participants in the festival. The Deity fined the Senior Okomfo of the festival for not having clothes for him to wear. When the Okomfo came out of possession the elders in attendance deemed that he had offended the Senior Okomfo in the most profound way as he disrespected the festival's intention and requirements. It is a requirement that any Okomfo attending a festival must come with their sacred possession gear and a willingness to bring forth their Deity if the Deity wants to display for the energy and healing of the people in attendance. Since this was not done, the Okomfo involved was called by the Elders and fined. A very big argument ensued and the Okomfo left with his entourage with a burst of anger. Later that week during the festival, an emissary from the Okomfo came to set up an apology. He stated that they (the Shrine House) realized that a big offense had been committed first by the Senior Okomfo and then by the big argument during the sacred event on sacred ground. A time was set for the apology and the fine was not changed. The apology had to be done in front of all who were in attendance at the festival in order that their Deities could also be appeased. Ultimately this was done prior to the closing of the festival. A special purification ritual was held to clean the Shrines and the people in attendance.

Procedures for Peers

Peers may approach each other directly or they can use an emissary the same as the previous category. It depends on the relationship of those involved. It is always a good idea to know that when offenses occur there may be some resentment or anger harbored by the offended. Thus it is not a bad idea to initially use an emissary to test the waters before approaching the offended. Sometimes the offender does not know that they have offended a person and is only made aware by the actions of the person or a comment from someone close to the offended. In that case, it is always good to send an emissary. This emissary could be an elder or another peer to open the door for the apology.

Peers usually present a dozen eggs accompanied by a drink. The apology is made directly to the individual and issues are resolved. Again, once the apology is accepted, it should not be discussed or brought up again.

Chapter 7

CELEBRATIONS AND SACRED DAYS

As most of us know, people of African descent love to celebrate and this is not stereotyping, it is fact. Our Ancestors, in the Akan culture, set aside special times to recognize each important occasion. These celebrations were properly planned and executed with all the appropriate protocols in place. Since these occasions were recognized as state mandated events, members of the community were not expected to go to regular jobs but to participate in the preparations for the celebrations. Celebrations were both Spiritual and political and were certainly a major social event. People traveled far and wide, in the country and on some occasions internationally, to attend these events.

In today's culture, these same ancient celebrations are still recognized and attended by those who are living abroad. Since there are so many of these events throughout the country we will highlight diverse celebration so that you can have an idea of how important our ancient system really is. Some of the celebrations we will discuss are Odwira or Yam festivals, birthdays, engagements, weddings, naming ceremonies, durbars, enstoolments, installations, and funerals. The very sacred days such as the Holy Days of each of the Deities, a time for honoring our Ancestors called Akwasiadae, annual festivals for the Deities, Akom Kese which is a state festival to honor Deities of the State and the leadership will be discussed. Just as there may be 77 Deities in each town, village, state, there are also celebrations of many types for each town, village and state which was practiced by our Ancestors and are continued today.

In the Diaspora, many of these celebrations are being presented in various ways. There are adaptations due to the fact that, for the most part, African religious and political celebrations and sacred days are not officially recognized by our country. The necessary rituals associated with these celebrations are not permitted in most places, and most employers refuse to authorize neither the liberal, administrative nor holiday leave that the Jewish, Catholic, Muslim and some other religions enjoy. However, in as much as we are known to be some of the most creative people in the world, the Akan communities in the Diaspora have created ways to make these celebrations as authentic as possible. Thus, the celebrations and sacred days that are discussed in this book are indeed celebrated in the Diaspora.

CELEBRATIONS

Akom Kese

Akom Kese is both a spiritual and political celebration. This event is held to announce an important Spiritual event or when an important Spiritual leader is visiting. Examples of this are the establishment of a new Shrine house, and an Okomfo graduation, also a political event including a religious component, which occurs when an Okomfo from Ghana visits the United States. At such an event, many other Shrine houses are invited to attend with their Akom orchestras. The focus of this event is on the displaying of Deities. The Okomfo Panyin arrives with their trainees, members, and other courtiers. You will see the elder women who are experienced in the preparation and serving of the food for the Deities; there are special seating arrangements according to rank and status.

There are occasions when a grand Spiritual celebration is performed. Those occasions might be a visiting Okomfo Panyin, Okomfohene, Akomfo, Spiritual leader. Traditional rulers whose past includes ritual leader, state rituals, death and funeral of an Okomfo, marriage of an Okomfo or any special occasion to honor an Okomfo and their patron Deity.

The Okomfohene, Akomfo, Akom drummers and singers, and Bosomfie members attend the Akom Kese (Big Akom). The Bosomkorafo, Gyegyefo, and other Shrine members including the Elder women and men are very important to the entourage as they participate in the preparation and serving of food to the Deities. The Shrine Akyeame who know how to serve particular Deities, and Abrafo who are also very knowledgeable about the sacrifices and other duities related to feeding the Deities are in attendance. They usually assist the hosts with the sacred work. In fact, the whole town, including those who may not agree with the traditional religion, turn out to watch this highly spiritual event. Not only do they watch, they also partake of the feast. Many miracles happen during the Akom Kese and there are fantastic displays of the Abosom in dress, dancing and singing.

The various Bosomfie (Shrine Houses) arrive in high spirits and with enthusiasm as the drums announce their arrival. Sometimes members of the non-initiated attendees are 'caught' by the Abosom and experience the energy short term. The are sometimes healed, decrease their doubt of the possession, and are called to the 'order'—to serve the Deity. In the latter instance, it is totally up to the individual to accept the 'call' or not. It is by choice of the individual. However, such a refusal may have consequences so that a visit to the shrine may become necessary to get out of the call without retribution.

Children especially like to attend these Akom Kese because the Deities that relate to children often display and favor them with candy and cookies. Likewise, women who need help in fertility, childbirth, marriage, etc. are present to ask assistance from special Deities. Men who are dealing with issues of impotence and other prostate problems invariably secretly come for help during the Akom Kese.

Durbar

Durbars are social and political events that are held to signify a special occurrence such as a Chief's anniversary, an international visiting dignitary or group visiting the regional palace and very often a visit by a political or government official. A State festival is also a time for a Durbar since the focus is on the achievements of the State and the incumbent Chief.

A Durbar is an opportunity for the Chief to invite all the Royals in the sur-rounding area, government officials, politicos, other dignitaries and special guests to the state. The number of VIPs who participate is a show of the popularity and the strength of the Chief, which is always of major importance to the state. The invited guests, especially the Chiefs and Queen Mothers, often arrive with a huge following which include their palace courtiers, the Chief Priest or Priestess and their entourage, as well as lay members of their community. The invitees are expected to arrive in their regalia with as large an entourage as manageable, which may consist of Abrafo, Linguists, the State Chief Priest and Okomfo Panyin, and other state courtiers. The regalia differs for each position, however one is likely to see ceremonial umbrellas, the state chair, stools, gorgeous entoma, sandals, head-gear, jewelry and other state implements. In Grand Durbars the Chief often rides in a palanquin. Attendees are dressed in their very best attire posturing and flaunting their regality and positions.

The State drums are played at a Durbar. The Chief's and Queenmother's arrival is announced by the state drum and he or she walks to the beat of the drum. Whenever a new Royal or special guest arrives, they too are announced by the State drum. The durbar is marked by the participation of cultural groups, brass bands, Okomfo displays, messages and speeches! There is a lot of dancing particularly the state dance such as Kete, Adowa, and ASAFO, and in some regions there are masqueraders who dance nonstop for as long as the brass band is playing. Sometimes the visitor is accompanied by a great contingency of Akomfo, which brings the expectation of an Akom during the Durbar. Or, a Chief might bring a retinue of the ASAFO Company, which means there will be an ASAFO display or competition if other companies are present. These activities spice up the program. Of all the celebrations, this is the most magnificent show of splendor, protocols, pomp and circumstance without apology. It is really an event to witness!

The Enstoolment and Outdoorings of Traditional Rulers

Enstoolments and outdoorings occur when an heir to an ancestral stool or a recognized position of honor and ruling is conferred on the appropriate individual. Enstoolments are both spiritual and political events. It is the marking or appointment of an individual to a position, which was previously vacated by death or otherwise. The public is invited to participate in this grand occasion. It signifies that the attached responsibility and related duties will now be duly executed.

The enstoolment requires the incumbent to undergo various secret as well as public Spiritual rituals and initiations. This is overseen by the Abusua Panyin or "head of the Family" and performed by an Okomfo.

In addition to inherited stools, a Chief has the flexibility of establishing honorary stools in his or her court based on a long list of traditional positions available to the village. The actual process of enstoolment may vary from region to region though some aspects are standard. For example, the Queenmother nominates the candidate. Then, the chosen individual is physically lifted in the air for all to see. Next, the person is secluded for a period of time to be taught lessons for the position. The newly enstooled is then given stool medicine for protection. Subsequently, the ruler is outdoored in the public and is expected to look, act, and perform like a traditional ruler.

The local and surrounding community turns out for the outdooring since it is not really known when or where the enstoolment will take place. There is plenty of drumming, dancing, singing, and revelry to mark the occasion. These rituals are performed by an Okomfo Panyin, Bosomfo and Abusua Panyin.

Engagements and Traditional Marriages

These are very special events in the line of life and death. It is believed that many rituals must be performed in order to insure the success of such unions. Therefore an Okomfo is again appointed to oversee these important rituals. For the continuation of the familial tribe, it is expected that each child marry. If that is not forthcoming, the family will take over and arrange for a marriage. If the person fails to carry through with the arrangement it is likely that the family will disinherit the person who refuses to live up to the family expectation. In ancient times, there was no choice in the matter. Nowadays, some children try to evade this responsibility for as long as possible, or may decide to select their own mate. In any event, the family must approve the marriage, or again disinheritance can take place.

It is believed that a marriage is the coming together of two families. Each family does its own detective work to explore family history, background, and character of the proposed person, wealth including property and other personal information about the individuals involved. After all has been done, then a serious courting ritual begins with the engagement that is considered the informal marriage. It is during this engagement that families expect that all the differences will be resolved between the couple. Then the marriage takes place.

Birthdays

The marking of a birthday is played down in the Akan society. It is not usually a public event. However, the mother plans a special dinner at which the immediate family attends. Eto is prepared for the celebrant with three eggs to signify their birth. The child, mother and father eat together. Libation is poured and well wishes are given. Those gathered talk about the birthday person. Sweets are given to the birthday person, which is very significant since sweets are not a part of the Ghanaian diet.

Sometimes but not often public rituals and sacrifices are done to thank the gods and the Ancestors. This is also a means of feeding the village participants because everyone gets to share in the sacrificial meat. Nothing is wasted. This is also a blessing to share in the foods given to the gods.

Funerals

This is one of the most sacred events in the community because it is these persons whose Spirits have made the transition to become our Ancestors. A funeral is both a Spiritual event and a major social event. It unfolds into two parts.

The funeral traditionally begins with wakekeeping on Friday night that continues until Noon on Saturday. Sometime before noon, customarily, the burial occurs. On Sunday, the thanksgiving service is held in church. There is much wailing before the person is buried. After which, the wailing stops and the celebration begins with music, cultural displays etc. There are also special songs sung and dances performed during a burial. Nowadays, when Christianity is becoming one of the dominant religions in Ghana, a preacher may be called to inter the body. This is when family conflict often flares up about how a person is laid to rest. These family conflicts are directly attributed to Christian beliefs, which have attempted to take precedence over the traditional customs of the Akans in Ghana.

The next year, or whenever the family can afford to do so, the official funeral is held, which is even more elaborate than the first. Funerals are taken very seriously and are very elaborate. Funerals are a celebration of life. Akans believe that the deceased person is in a better position to help the family so everyone gathers to celebrate that person's life. Special drums are used and special rhythms are played at funerals.

The Abusua Panyin presides over the burial and funeral rituals.

In the Diaspora, there may be similar family conflicts. Even though the deceased has practiced traditional Akan religion, many family members do not and will not allow the bereaved family to conduct a traditional funeral. In addition, uninitiated morticians will not understand the special needs for the rituals and ceremony that should be performed on the dead body and, must follow strict state laws. It can be quite a challenge with all of this working to compromise our beliefs. It is recommended that, in order to keep peace in the family during a time of mourning, the initiated in the family may need to conduct their rituals at a later time with believers, while still participating in the services that are most prevalent in their family. Of course, there are certain things that can be done to appease our Ancestors for this anomaly. More is written on the topic of funerals in the section on <u>Rituals and Rites of Passage.</u>

SACRED DAYS

We all celebrate some type of sacred or special day such as Easter, Christmas, Kwanzaa, civil rights achievements, heroes and sheroes. Every religion has several sacred days that are held in high esteem by its practitioners. It is the same with those who practice the Akan Akom Tradition. There are several sacred days on the Akan calendar. In Ghana and in the Diaspora, Akans take time to celebrate the sacred days or community holidays. The highest holy day on the Akan calendar is Akwasiadae.

Akwasiadae is celebrated every 40-42 days depending on the calendar day since it always held on Sunday, which in Twi is Kwasidae. This day is reserved for honoring our personal and community Ancestors. There are eight or nine during any calendar year depending on the number of Sundays in the year. The last Akwasiadae of the calendar year is the Big Adae or Adae Kese, which is given special attention in terms of food, life force offerings and participation.

In the Diaspora and in Ghana, we usually have a special Akom or gathering for Akwasiadae. During this celebration, there is drumming, dancing and singing of the songs of our Ancestors, which are also the songs of many of the Abosom. Eto, which is one of the most important foods of the Abosom and Nsamanfo, is cooked and shared. Eto is prepared with mashed white African yam, which is a root plant but not the sweet potato/yam that we in the Diaspora are accustomed to eating. Eto is prepared in two ways, the natural white and white that is reddened with palm oil. Hard-boiled eggs are added whole as a garnish making the Eto complete.

Everyone is encouraged to celebrate Akwasiadae as a means of maintaining contact with your Ancestors. The Ancestors form an important part of our pantheon trilogy. They are also known as the old people or ancient people. Akans believe in life after death therefore when a person's body dies their Spirit lives on. The Ancestors are loved and respected. We believe that they are with us and are always looking out for us. They ensure that we follow protocols that have been established. The Ancestors are always protecting us and opening doors for us even though we may not consciously recognize their work. According to our traditional beliefs, the Ancestors are in close contact with Almighty God, thus we can call on them for assistance.

Just as we visit the cemetery to place flowers on the graves of our loved ones on holidays such as Easter, Mother's Day, Father's Day, Veterans Day, Birthdays, and the anniversary of their death, we can also add this special celebration. This also creates an opportunity to bring family, close friends and community together. During this very personal celebration you should serve Eto. In addition, you should also prepare the favorite meal of one of your Ancestors to share with those present. Place some on your Ancestral altar to be eaten after a short period of time. If you do not know your Ancestors, you can prepare any special meal and share it with those present. Display pictures of your Ancestors. Sing some of their favorite songs and share stories about them. You probably have other ideas about this celebration, which is your event and can be whatever you want it to be. Just bring it from the heart and your Ancestors will acknowledge your efforts.

Wukudae or Little Adae as it is commonly known is another Holy Day on the Akan calendare. It is celebrated on the Wednesday that falls every 40-42 days. Awukudae is celebrated primarily in the Eastern Region. It is said that the Nsamanfo and other shrines are roaming about to ensure that tradition and custom is being held. On this day, the focus is on the Nsamanfo shrines that are fed special food along with the other Shrines. Awukudae is also a day for charitable causes. Bosomfie members feed the hungry, make donations towards any good causes, and visit the sick. In the village, anyone who wants to eat

Akomfo do not travel on Awukudae, unless absolutely necessary. It is said to be a dangerous day for Akomfo to travel, so they stay home unless it becomes absolutely necessary to travel. It is a highly emotional day when families are feeding ancestors and trying to resolve issues. Thus, Akomfo stay close to their stations in order to avoid confrontations, reduce the risk of tragedies and to receive any messages that might be brought by the Shrines regarding family matters and order.

Fofie or Bad Day, is another Holy Day on the Akan calendar that is celebrated primarily among Tegare Shrines. It is believed that Tegare's "eyes are red"

meaning he is on a great mission. He is roaming about doing his work of hunting and catching evil doers and liars. Akomfo do not leave their stations on this day, unless absolutely necessary, as they do not want to get caught in the crossfire. On this day, specific rituals and sacrifices are performed. This day also occurs every 40-42 days on a Friday.

SACRED DAYS FOR AKAN DEITIES AND MORE...

There are many Sacred and Holy days on the Akan calendar. Many of them are aligned with the Abosom and Ancestors. On these days, Akomfo and practitioners of the Akan Akom Tradition most likely do special rituals and sacred work. Following are some examples that by no means are exhaustive.

Sunday

In addition to celebrating Akwasiadae every 40-42 days, Nana Asuo Gyebi's Holy Day is Sunday. **Nana Asuo Gyebi** is a male Abosom. He is the patron deity of Asomdwee Fie and the national deity of the Akans in America. Nana Asuo Gyebi is an ancient river deity. He is a great healer and protector. Nana Asuo Gyebi is known to have come to America to help the lost children of Africa reclaim their Spiritual inheritance. Nana Asuo Gyebi is also the Obrafo to Nana Panyin, who is the head of the Akan pantheon. Nana Asuo Gyebi is known to like gifts of White Horse Scotch, J&B Scotch, peanuts in the shell, green bananas, white rice, grits, and corned beef.

Tuesday

Nana Esi Ketewaa is known as the Mother of the Akan Shrines in Ghana and the Diaspora. She is a deified ancestor who died while in childbirth. She is a protector of children and women. Women often seek her assistance and protection during and after childbirth. She has a motherly nature and helps anyone who seeks her assistance. Nana Esi is also the Okyeame to Nana Panyin. Nana Esi loves to receive gifts of Fanta orange soda, fruity wines, eggs, yams, honey, candy, sugar cane, and white cloth. She also enjoys gifts of flowers, colorful scarves, and perfume.

In some regions in Ghana, it is a taboo to fish on Tuesday. It is believed that the gods of the Sea are walking around and do not want to be disturbed. The risk is to offend them and become a sacrifice. This is a very important day for visitors to remember. While I was in Ghana, a visiting person from the US wanted to experience the sea…just put their feet into the sea from the vantage point of a rock. The sea sucked the person in and that person was found 2 days later and obviously the fish had started to eat the flesh and the body had been thrown against the rocks. It was a sad occasion but a reminder to honor the various customs in the country in which you are visiting.

Thursday

Thursday is a sacred day to **Asase Yaa** or Mother Earth. On that day, there is no farming in most regions of Ghana. No one is buried on that day. No planting or harvesting on that day. And, there are many other restrictions associated with Mother Earth depending on the region involved. There are some religions and tribes that do not honor this taboo.

Friday

Nana Panyin appears early Friday mornings and leaves before sunrise. She is justice and rules with an iron hand. I will mention her full name for the purpose of information in this book; however, we do not use her name lightly and routinely. Nana Abena Akonedi is a very powerful, left-handed Deity who is not to be played with. When she displays, she wears all white and is very elegant in her dancing. Her persona is very calm and has an aura of power. Most people, even those who don't know her, shake in her very presence. No one wants to have any unfinished business when she comes. Nana Panyin likes foreign or imported Schnapps, money, and white cloth.

This is also a sacred day for **Nana Adade Kofi** who is the messenger for Nana Panyin. Whenever Nana Panyin wants to send an important last warning, she will send Adade Kofi. This is important when people come to her for settling cases and disputes. There was a particular land dispute associated with a funeral in Ghana. The two families could not come to an agreement and decided to take the case to Nana Panyin to ask her to settle the dispute. This was done only after much negotiation and stalemates. Nana Panyin told the people to settle the dispute among themselves. If she settled it they might not like the outcome and her ruling would be final. Anyone who went against the case would be severely punished or die. She waited for the families to come together with a decision and they went back and forth. Some even started crying. Adade Kofi came and fined both the families severely and wanted the money and sheep immediately because they had angered Nana Panyin. After receiving the offerings, he warned them to settle in a few minutes or Nana Panyin would rule. Within five minutes of that message the two families settled the dispute. It was awesome to witness. Because they took up the Okomfo's time and energy they had to pay the Okomfo heavily.

Adade Kofi is a male Deity and is known for his physical strength and perserverance. He is a Deity of iron, metals and is a warrior. Nana Adade Kofi is also the youngest son of Nana Panyin. Adade Kofi usually displays immediately after Nana Panyin comes early Friday mornings. In fact, he might appear at anytime just to show his strength and to report what's going on to Nana Panyin. Nana Adade Kofi loves to receive gifts of eggs, palm wine, white rice and white cloth.

Friday is a very important day for **Nana Tegare**, who is a defied ancestor. He is said to be from Northern Ghana who settled throughout Ghana, Ivory Coast, Togo and other places in West Africa. Tegare is a hunter who seeks truth, exposes witches, liars, thieves and evildoers. Tegare is a healer who is very skilled in the identification and use of herbs. He protects and helps anyone who asks. Also there are many other well-known Deities within the Tegare system. When Tegare displays he wears northern Ghana type clothing which is primarily Muslim attire. He wears a Batakari, knickers or pants, sometimes carries prayer beads, akonti or some other kind of hunter's stick. He is a skilled dancer and loves to dance high life which is a fast and fancy dance. People love to dance with Nana Tegare and he is fun loving. However, even though he may be laughing and telling jokes, one must be very careful for he is usually giving messages at the same time. He loves to tell "truths" about anyone who may be present. Nana Tegare enjoys gifts of money, pipes and pipe tobacco, cigarettes, cigars, kola nuts, beer, schnapps, rum, and tiger nuts.

Saturday

The day before Akwasiadae is a very important day to remember. It is called Dapaa. It is the day that cleaning takes place in order for the Ancestors to be welcomed into the space. Thus, the altars and Shrines are cleaned. Everything is dusted and moved, swept and made ready for the celebration

This is only a partial list of sacred days and a representation of some of the Deities that are a part of the Diasporan pantheon, meaning those Deities that have chosen to cross the waters to protect and minister to the lost children of Africa.

FESTIVALS

Festivals Sponsored by the State

There are many important festivals in Ghana. Some are State festivals that are primarily political. However, all festivals have a spiritual component, which entails weeks of sacred rituals, some of which are held prior to, during and after the festival. There are also very popular festivals which are held for specific Deities.

One well-known State sponsored festival is called the Odwira Festival is similar to the New Year's celebration here in the US. However, this celebration is more than one day and there are other differences. Odwira is celebrated in all of the farming regions of Ghana to celebrate the harvesting of new crops. There are regional differences regarding the rituals however preparation for the Odwira festival is very similar. Prior to the start of the Odwira, all members of the community are obligated to settle any lingering disputes and resolve issues. In the Akan community, there is a very clear system for resolving issues, conflicts and misunderstandings among the people. It is expected that each member of the village use these systems to maintain a level of peace and prosperity in the village. It is believed that in order to receive blessings in the upcoming year, every attempt must be made to settle outstanding issues. In Akan culture, disputes, conflicts and messy issues tend to anger the Gods and Ancestors of the village who are adamant about keeping the ancient laws, customs and traditions that maintained order and brought blessings to the village. There is always the possibility of retribution in the form of sickness, drought, non-productive farming, not enough fish, sluggish business, no new children born and other serious calamities that can occur in the village.

Additionally, there is a huge cleanup process in the village palace, individual houses, and Shrines prior to Odwira. This is all a part of the ritual of bringing in the New Year. Though the timelines for the rituals may differ slightly by region, usually Odwira begins on Sunday when libation is poured at a sacred place at the Chief's palace or in some other designated sacred place in the village. This libation is poured to thank the Gods and Ancestors of the village for helping to resolve all of the conflicts of the past year, those that are unresolved to aid in the appropriate resolutions, and to ask for blessings and less conflict for the coming years. Each day has order and special rituals are observed. During this time, the Spirit which is the protector and provider of the village is on display. State stools are ritually washed during Odwira. Purification ceremonies are performed for the entire community including the Chief, Queenmother, Elders and other members of the Traditional Royal Council.

Following is a partial list of some other annual festivals that are conducted by the State under the auspices of the Chief. All of these festivals have major spiritual components, which require traditional rituals such as libation, sacrificial offerings, and other ceremonies specific to the region, which are performed by the State. These rituals and ceremonies are similar to those described above with rituals that are specifically connected to the State Deities. Usually, the work is done by the State Okomfo. The list of State sponsored festivals is quite extensive and can be obtained from the Ghana Tourism Bureau.

State Sponsored Festivals

Aboakyir	May	Winneba
Bakatue	1st Tuesday in July	Elmina
Damba Festival	June/July	Tamale/Yendi
Agogo Afahye	August	Agogo
Kente Festival	August	Bonwire
Yaa Asantewaa Fest.	August	Ejisu & Kumasi
Homowo Festival	August/September	Accra
Fetu Afahye	1st Sat. in September	Cape Coast
Kundum Festival	Sept/October	Western Region

| Odwira | October | Akwapim Region |
| Edina Bronya | December/January | Elmina |

Festivals for the Deities

In addition to the Odwira and other State celebrations, there are festivals, which are directly related to particular Abosom. These festivals are held to give honor and thanks to the Deities and Ancestors for their many blessings. These festivals are sponsored and financed by the various Shrines; however, the State often makes some type of contribution such as food stuffs, life force offerings, drinks, and money. Very often representatives of the Ahenfie are sent to participate in the celebration. Festivals typically last for several days with a huge celebration on the last day. There is traditional drumming, dancing and singing. The Deities are fed specific sacred food, life force offerings are given to the Deities, plus the Shrines and implements are cleaned. Invitations are sent to other Shrine houses with the traditional drink attached. It is typical for people in the surrounding towns who are not invited to attend during the festival to offer their energy and support. The festivals last all night with little sleep by attendees. It is a highly charged and energized event and similar to having an all night, all week Akom!

For example, immediately following the Odwira in Akwapim, the Nana Panyin festival is held in Larteh followed by the Nana Panyin festivals held by other Nana Panyin Okomfo in different towns and villages. These are held from October through December. January begins the Nana Asuo Gyebi Festivals, the first of which is held in Larteh followed by others put on by various Nana Asuo Gyebi Okomfo. Nana Panyin is considered to be the head of the pantheon of Deities in the Akwapim area in the Eastern Region of Ghana. In addition, she is recognized as the head of the Pantheon of all the Deities in Ghana. Each region, town or village has a Deity that is designated the head of that region, town or village. These Shrines must be fed and appeased annually, in addition to other rituals performed during the year. The duration of most of these festivals is 7-10 days in which the Okomfo who is responsible for the maintenance and upkeep of the Shrine does not leave the village. Specific ancient rituals have been established for each festival. The Okomfo Panyin is responsible for conducting those rituals in the proper sequence and format. Life force offerings have been designated for each deity, special food is prepared for each Deity, and of course there is much singing and dancing in the Akan Akom Tradition.

Festival Components

I will share with you some of the components of the festival for Nana Panyin. However, this is not a comprehensive description of the rituals that are conducted during this time.

Nana Panyin's festival begins at midnight Thursday night when the ritual fire is ignited. Nana Panyin arrives to inspect that fire and to assure participants that she acknowledges that everything is in order and thus, the festival can begin. She stays only a short time. Immediately after she leaves, Nana Adade Kofi appears briefly and displays as the songs related to him are sung. Friday morning, between 3am and 4 am, Nana Panyin arrives again to bring messages and to dance. Later that day, the food is cooked for the Nsamanfo associated with the Shrine.

On Saturday after the new yams have been released to the people, a special food called Yoma, which is pronounced "yooo ma", is prepared using the head of the Ram that was given to Nana Panyin. Yoma is prepared in a special manner with Eto and eggs.

Sunday is the party for Nana Esi which includes cookies, sugar cane, bread, rice, candy, ground nuts, cakes, banana, coconut, Fanta orange minerals, Gin, and wine. The Nana Esi Okomfo will make tea and rice for Nana Esi with chicken as she does not like other meats and does not like fufu.

Monday is a display of all Deities who decide to make an appearance while regular cooking with the new yams is accomplished. The singing, dancing and drumming only stop when the people take a break to eat. The celebration resumes after the eating.

Tuesday Nana Panyin appears early in the morning if she has something to say. There is special food for that day. Eto is served every day.

On Wednesday morning, Nana Asuo Gyebi who is the Obrafo to Nana Panyin is the main Deity who will display along with other Deities.

The last day is Thursday when the ashes from the ritual fire, which has been burning since the first day, any remaining fire, palm wine, the peelings from the yams, plantain peelings, egg shells and other items are gathered. Before midnight, these items are taken to Nana Esi's village. At the village, we sing Nana Esi songs; she will probably come, as the items are being dumped into the river. An Okomfo will possess Nana Esi as libation is poured in thanksgiving. When returning no one looks back, or it is believed that someone will become ill because Nana Esi is walking behind you which is normally a taboo. Later in the early morning, which is the time that Nana Panyin always appears, She will possess an Okomfo and give final messages.

In Ghana, work is suspended during this time and acknowledged by employers. In Ghana, no one has to worry about losing a job or be concerned about having to face some other punitive action. In fact, employers often send offerings or some even attend at least one night of this exciting event. Conversely, in the Diaspora, it is highly unlikely that a festival will last all week long with the attendance very high. Believers must take leave from their jobs or may experience punitive actions by their employers. Usually, the festivals are celebrated over the weekend.

Chapter 8

RITUALS AND RITES OF PASSAGE

Rituals are performed for almost every important occasion in the Akan community. Rituals are necessary for those who believe in the traditional methods of communicating with the Abosom and Ancestors. Rituals keep the doors open to the Spirit world in order to receive clear guidance, direction, and messages that enable us to live peaceful, prosperous, and healthy lives. Rituals help with the process of transforming our minds, body and Spirits from the notions of false or negative beliefs, thoughts and actions to the customs, traditions, beliefs, attitudes, behaviors, and actions which have been ordained by our ancient Ancestors. Those teachings enabled our most recent Ancestors of the Middle Passage to survive the inhumane treatment and subsequent enslavement in the Diaspora. Consequently they were able to salvage those ancient wisdom teachings despite the efforts to eradicate all remnants of our existence.

Most Akan rituals have survived in their entirety; some have been adapted because of incompatible conditions in the Diaspora. Akan rituals involve various aspects of nature, personal objects, scents and/or various herbs. They are conducted by appropriate members of the community. For example, the Abusua Panyin, or head of the family might conduct a family ritual; the Asafohene/hema will lead a ritual for the Asafo Company. The Chief, who may deputize the Chief Priest of the village to carry out the ritual, will lead the community or village ritual. The village Shrine rituals are conducted by the Chief Priest, Bosomfo, or another Senior Okomfo of the village. Rituals for the women and children of the village may be conducted by a male or female Okomfo, the Queenmother or Obaa Panyin.

The rituals may be a one time event or recurring event. The duration varies according to the custom or the need as dictated by the guardian Deities of the village.

Libation

Libation is the singularly most important ritual that is conducted in the Akan community. It is an integral part of Akan life. It is a form of prayer, communication and unifying connection between those on earth with Onyame, the Abosom and the Ancestors of the Spirit world. Libation expresses a belief in God and the various Deities in the traditional pantheon of lesser gods and Ancestors.

Libation confirms that we are aware that we are not self-sufficient but depend on God, and the Spirits on a higher plane to intercede for us in every part of our life. In addition, it is an acknowledgement of our belief in life after death…knowing that there is another world which we call Asamando where the Spirits reside.

The order of libation clearly explains our belief that God is Almighty as that is the first appellation to be voiced, followed by the Asase Yaa who is second in power, followed by the Abosom and Nsamanfo. Drink is offered during libation, however no drink is offered to God, rather we acknowledge that God has made everything including this way of praying. Another important result of libation is that active participants feel a connection to the community of like-minded individuals, which furthers the faith in the process and a sense of family and extended family. It acknowledges the common belief system of those present and those who have transcended.

Akomfo pour libation at Akoms and other religious services. The Okyeame or Linguist pours libation when a Royal is sitting in State. Elders of the family pour libation to their Ancestors for the enrichment of the entire family. Both men and women pour libation. I have been asked about children pouring libation. It is strongly believed that children under the age of puberty do not have the in depth knowledge of the purpose and components of libation. Therefore they are not permitted to pour libation in public. Sometimes the family will allow a child who has passed puberty and is being taught the necessary components of the ritual to pour libation in the home. Usually only the family is present on these rare occasions. They would not pour libation at a public event or forum. The only exception would be in an artistic performance and most times the libation component is not included in the play rather it is preferred before the performance begins.

Libation is poured at the beginning of all important occasions to ask blessings, guidance, protection, and peace during the event. All important agreements are sealed with libation for this is considered an oath before God, the Abosom and Ancestors. Most libations ask for more children in the family because that is the way our culture continues. Though similar in the initial components, libation is a time that the person pouring libation displays their finesse, skill and knowledge of appropriate proverbs and important events in the community. The more flourishes, intonations, modulations and proverbs used, the more accolades the person receives. Libation is usually poured while offering a drink to the Abosom and

Ancestors. Drink is not offered to God. However, it is offered to Asase Yaa who is considered to be second to God.

Festivals and other ritual ceremonies are very special occasions that call for the use of prayers. Libation can be poured at anytime one seeks the blessings and guidance of higher powers such as before one eats, when one feels the need for Spiritual guidance, upliftment or when one visits a shrine for Spiritual direction. Akan families use libation to maintain constant contact with their Ancestors who are members of the extended family. It is a family obligation to maintain this contact because the Ancestors are the Spirits that guide us in customs, traditions, and appropriate behavior. The Ancestors are the keepers of the tradition and are the ones who check us when things are out of order.

Following is an example of a general Libation, which you may use until you are comfortable enough to add or change it. Remember to do this with some style. You will need to learn some Akan proverbs to really be impressive.

General Libation

Onyame, Almighty God, I call you because it is you alone who has established this system whereby I can be in close contact with my Ancestors. I acknowledge that in all things you have the ultimate power over everything that I do or ask. I know that you are with me, around me and have established your system of Ancestral Spirits for me. Thank you for my life, my health and my strength. I also thank you for my family.

Asase Yaa: Mother Earth, the one who provides sustenance for us everyday all day. I call you. *Nsa*

I call all the **rivers and waters** associated with me, my family, and my Ancestors:

Potomac River	Nsa
Ohio River	Nsa
Absecon River	Nsa
Volta River	Nsa

Mavis Bank River	Nsa

Now I wish to call all of my Ancestors.

Momma Helen	Nsa
Cousin Chris	Nsa
Auntie Tine	Nsa
Uncle JoeB.	Nsa

I call all of my Ancestors who I may not know who are willing to assist me in my journey on this earth.

Nsa

This is (your name) calling you to commune with me for a little while. First of all, thank you for all the doors that you have opened for me. Thanks for my new job with a raise. Thank you giving me guidance in that situation I mentioned to you before. Thanks for helping the children in school...their grades are improving.... (Nsa)

I know that you continue to lookout for me. I am asking you just to help me have peace of mind in these situations and challenges before me. (Nsa) Help me to maintain order and understanding of my role in life.(Nsa) Help me to continue on my Spiritual path and to do those things to help me and my family to grow.(Nsa)

Nananom, I know that you will do this for me. And, I thank you for your assistance.

Yooooooooooooooo. (Pour out all of the drink)

Akan Rites of Passage

Akan Rites of Passage mark important transitions. Proper rituals are conducted for each to ensure success in the outcome of those transitional periods. All of the rituals are conducted based on the traditions and customs set by Ancestors and passed on orally by the Elders in the community who are designated to oversee these rituals. Some of the rites of passage are listed below which include some examples of rituals performed during those ceremonies. Those rites of passage listed are related to life, life transitions and death.

Edin To Rites (Naming Ceremony)

Akans believe that the success of an individual depends on the way their life is ushered into this planet. When the potential mother becomes pregnant certain very private rituals are performed to make certain that the baby is protected while in the womb of the woman. In addition, it is a time that an attempt to determine whether or not the baby will stay for a while or not. Sometimes it is revealed sometimes it is not revealed. The Abusua Panyin or Chief Priest of the village performs this ritual.

Once delivery begins, there are women in the village who attend to this precious and important re-entry of an ancestor into the community. All women are not permitted to witness this occasion because of the importance of the event…only those who are trained to follow the protocols established by Ancestors are allowed attendance. Midwifery is a very honorable and important position in the Akan community. It carries the same if not more importance of that of a medical doctor because this represents the continuation of the clan.

As soon as the baby is born, certain rituals are performed for both the mother and the child. The day the child is born is noted, as well as the time and the position of the planets. This all is used to determine the destiny the child has chosen. This child is presented to the father and the grandparents and select close members of the family. On the eighth day, if the child survives, it is known that the child has elected to stay for a while to accomplish the tasks it has agreed with Odomankoma to accomplish while on this planet.

Thus, a naming ceremony takes place in the privacy of the father's compound or the Abusua Shrine. At this time the child is given its name by the father. Three names are given: the day name which is the day that the baby was born; the second name may be that of a prominent ancestor such as the deceased grandfather, grandmother, aunt, uncle, or other family member and the placement name in the family. For example, if the child is the 3rd born, that child will have the name Mensal attached to denote the 3rd born. Or if there are twins, there is a different kind of ritual and the children are named Panyin (the first to be born) and Ata (the second to be born). Another variation to the naming is if something peculiar or a special event occurred during the pregnancy, such as if the mother had previous miscarriages or the baby was born but died at birth or few days after. Clearly, this is a peculiar event and the baby is often given a name such as Donkor, or marks on the face that would deter the event from happening again. During this naming ceremony, the child is given instructions as to what is expected as a productive family member and community member. This ceremony is called the "Edin To". Following is an example of an Edin To ceremony. A similar public ceremony is usually held after 8 weeks so that the community can see the child and give well wishes and present a start up fund for the child.

On the early morning of the eighth day, the father, Abusua Panyin, uncle or Okomfo will gather with the family at the appropriate place. Early morning means dawn which is before the moon descends and the sun rises. The child who is naked but wrapped in a receiving blanket is brought outside to face the morning sun rising.

Libation is poured to the Ancestors to ask permission to proceed with the naming ceremony. The father of the child then whispers the name that he has chosen into the child's ear so that the child is the first to hear the name. It is then given to the person conducting the ceremony and that person announces it to those close family members who are attending the ceremony. Then the one who is conducting the ceremony uses water and another clear beverage to conduct a simple but very important ceremony. At that time, each beverage in turn is placed on the lips of the child to allow the child to know the difference and the child is told to always know the difference between a lie and the truth. The child is encouraged to always tell the truth. The child is also given the explanation of their name, day name, and the attributes of the ancestor that he/she is named after. The expectation of the behavior in concert with expectations of a good citizen of the community is explained to the child. It is at this time that the destiny of the new born, which has been determined according to the day, time and position of the planets surrounding its birth, is also explained to the child.

Appropriate songs are sung led by Nana Esi Ketewaa songs. Some people even dance during this time for it is a celebration of life. Everything that is done at this time during this celebration is directed towards the child. Thus, an Akan child gets its direction very early in life and is reminded of this by those present if later he/she should veer from their chosen path. The father, mother, uncles and aunts are given their responsibilities in relation to the child. The ceremony and ritual ends with everyone partaking of the drink used for the instruction of the child. A meal is usually served and the family members disperse before the rest of the community is aware that this has all occurred.

The public ceremony is held after the child is 8 weeks old. This is the occasion where the child is outdoored to the community. It is quite similar to the initial ceremony. However, the mother and baby are dressed up in the traditional manner with powder or clay on the skin to denote a sacred state. The initial ceremony is repeated for the community to see and hear. A very important addition to this public outdooring is that during this ceremony, the community members pledge their support for the child. This is usually a very moving ceremony as people step forward to announce their pledges and to present gifts. Merrymaking and celebration in the form of music, dance and feasting, of course, follow this.

Akan Soul Names
(Also referred to as Day Names)

(Fante/Twi Language)

Day of the week	Male Name	Female Name
Sunday	Kwesi/Kwasi	Esi/Asi/Akosua
Monday	Kodwo/Kojo/Kwadwo	Adwoa/Adjowa
Tuesday	Kobena/Kwabena	Araba/Abena
Wednesday	Kweku/Kwaku	Ekua/Ekuwa/Akua
Thursday	Kwaw/Yaw/Yao	Aba/Yaa
Friday	Kofi	Efua/Efuwa/Afua
Saturday	Kwame/Kwamena/Kwamina	Amma/Amba/Ama

The only time that these day names are not used is when the child is being named after an ancestor giving the full name of the ancestor, i.e., Nana Yaw Abaka. Perhaps the child was born on Sunday, however this is later explained to the child because the personality of a Sunday child will be evident in the characteristics of the child.

Following is a chart for sequential births. These names can be applied along with the day name preceding this name. When this occurs, the child is most often called by the sequential name.

Sequence	Male	Female
First Born	Abakah	Abaka
Third Born	Mensah	Mansa
Seventh Born	Esuon	Ason
Eighth	Awotwe	same
Ninth	Nkruma	same
Tenth	Badu	same
Twins	Ata	Ataa
Triplets	N'taansa	same
After Twins or Triplets	Tawia	same
Next Child after Tawia	Abam	same
Next	Nyakomagow	same
Next	Nyameboe	Etuakesan
Child born after a mis-carriage	Donkor	Donkor

Sequential Names (Fante Language)

Elders recently informed me that some of the names I had been hearing were not just someone's name but were associated with day names. These names were considered 'family favorite names,' or as we call them, nicknames. Most people are not called these names outside of the home or with relatives. For example, unless I am related to a person or on a very familiar basis with the person, I would not use their home name. So, Ekua would always be Ekua, unless I am family or a very close friend of the family or grew up in that person's home and therefore considered a sister or brother.

Soul Appellations or Family Favorite Names

Week Day Name	Appellation	Other Names	Appellation
Kwesi	Ebueakwan	Nkrumah	Egyaefi
Esi	Odanyin	Atta	Owosaw
Kodwo	Asere	Abaka	Sikanyi
Adwoa	Adae	Appea	Kubi
Kobena	Ebo	Ofori	Amanfo
Araba	Danso	Ansa	Sesreku
Kweku	Abaeku	Kwansa	Opirim
Ekua	Enyampa		
Kwaw	Operba		
Aba	Gyakye		
Kofi	Ntsiful		
Efua	Nkoso		
Kwamena	Ato		
Ama	Adoma		

Ye Gora BraRites (Girls Puberty Rites)

Rituals are held to mark the onset of menses that is the entry to womanhood for young girls, which usually happens around the age of 12 or 13. These rituals are performed by the female elders in the family and designated female elders from the community. The girls receive lessons on womanhood, self-esteem, sex education and customs, role as a woman, dealing with men, their responsibilities within the home, presentation and public behavior and other expectations. This education happens in seclusion for 7-14 days at which time the initiate receives Spiritual baths and traditional medicine to ward off evil Spirits, for enlightenment, protection and to usher in their reproductive cycle. During this period of time, they are taught songs and dances related to their new status which are all instructional. In some areas, the initiate's head is shaved in other areas a special hair style is given.

At the end of the seclusion, they are outdoored in large community celebration showing their elevation to womanhood in which they are topless and displaying their physical goods as the dance and sing the songs learned during their seclusion. The community then offers gifts and support as they offer words of wisdom, admonishments and encouragement for young ladies. The end of this formal ceremony, they are dressed up in beads, which signify wealth and prosperity, fine cloth wrapped in traditional styles and ohenaba's or traditional sandals, and dangling earrings. Of course there is a celebratory meal served by the family members and community.

The next day, the initiates are ushered around the community from door to door to announce they are of age and to thank those who have contributed to the rituals and/or someway formally or informally to their upbringing thus far. Of course, this is the traditional way of ushering in womanhood, which many communities have dropped because of the great expense associated with this type of celebration. However, the family is obligated to do something even on a much smaller scale.

Rites of Passage for Boys

A formal rites of passage for boys does not exist among the Akans as it does in some other tribes in Ghana.

Prior to puberty, they boy is the responsibility of the mother. She nurtures him and teaches him as only a mother can. However, from the onset of puberty, it is the responsibility of the uncle of the boy to make certain that they know and are following proper protocols. They are schooled on responsibilities of becoming a young man. They are given tests of endurance, taught how to dress well, and continue their education of hot to interact with women as well as their peers.

During this time, the young boys are also taught the family history, their place in the family as well as the family trade. For example, some families are known for their skills as drummers, carpenters, masons, etc. The young boys are expected to learn something of the family trade. Some boys, however, do not follow the trade of the family and only give answers and appears to pay attention in order to placate their elders.

Thus, **the Elders say:** *"When you teach a boy, you teach a person; but when you teach a girl, you educate a nation."*

Aweregye Rites (Marriage Ceremony) and Engagement

The coming together of two families is a very important ritual in the life of an Akan. Therefore the rituals of engagement and marriage are taken very seriously and nothing is left to guessing. Of course, in today's modern society some things are changing such as a move to openness in relationships. However, Akans still frown upon outward public displays of affection between two lovers. It is assumed if you are hugging or kissing a person on the cheek that it is a very good friend and not a lover. Usually, in a public setting you can only see the evidence of a relationship through rings or who sits next to whom or some other innocuous gesture. The intimate hugs and kisses that are freely displayed in the Diaspora are considered taboo. Those taboos are still recognized and practiced.

Another major taboo is that one should not marry a first, second, or third cousin. Since the word cousin is not a part of the Akan family structure, it would be as if the person was marrying their sister or brother. This causes families and suitors to delve deeply into their family history and clans to ensure that there is no breech of this taboo.

Engagement

Following is an example of the Akan engagement process.

It is the responsibility of the man to approach the family in a custom known as "knocking". This is done by going to the family to express a personal interest in the family. The man goes to the family with a drink to introduce himself and holds a general conversation and then leaves.

The second time the individual goes "knocking" with a drink, it is at a pre-arranged time. The occasion is well orchestrated. The man does not go alone but with his father, uncles and other male elders of the family. The father or uncle does all of the talking. The pursuer cannot talk to the girl's father directly.

During Amonee, the drink is presented with a small amount of money and the reason for the visit is announce which is that the "*the man is seeking permission to become engaged to the woman*". Of course, the family becomes animated and suspicious. The negotiations begin and the questions are rapidly fired off. What are they bringing to the table? How will they compensate the family for the loss of the services of the girl who will be leaving the mother? How can they trust the individual to take care of the girl? What financial means does the pursuer's family have? What financial means does the man have? What type of job does he hold? Meanwhile, after the first visit, the female's family has already begun their research into the pursuer's family, history, background and all other needed information. They are asking these questions to find out if there is a liar in the house. The questions are systematically answered.

If satisfied, the family will ask which daughter the pursuer is interested in. They want to be sure that he knows the daughter. So a filing a parade of women, who may or may not look like the pursued, file past the man and he has the opportunity to say "yes, that's the one" or "no, that's not the one". Finally, he will select the correct woman. Next, his family has to present gifts and money to the woman. She must see what he is worth. Her family members are also checking out the gifts to determine if they are appropriate and if they are sufficient.

This event may require a full day of negotiations. At the end of the day, the man gets the appropriate woman and the party begins. They are now officially engaged. Everyone in the community must respect the relationship as if they were already married. It is only the marriage rituals and ceremony left that will probably take place within the next year.

Aweregye Rites (Marriage Ceremony)

An Okomfo, Chief, Queenmother or Elder performs the traditional marriage ceremony. It all depends on the wishes of the couple. Some couples opt for both a civil ceremony and a traditional ceremony which will be performed either before or after the civil ceremony. In any event, all or select traditional customs are performed.

When the engaged couple is to be married, the preparation is similar to the preparation of those of us in the Diaspora. There are meetings with family members, counseling of the couple by the person who will perform the ceremony. The entire community is involved in the marriage. There are special duties for the parents, male and female attendants. It is definitely a community activity. Two families are coming together and must support the marriage.

Again the intended husband must send an emissary to the woman's family to state his intention to marry. Negotiations are conducted on proper dowry and other gifts to satisfy the family members for the same reasons stated during the engagement ceremony. When this has been agreed upon, the invitations can go out to the guests. Following is an example of a traditional Akan ceremony.

The community participants assemble outside in the courtyard or a designated place outside of the actual ceremonial space. The men line up on the right side behind the groomsmen; women line up on the left side behind the Bridesmaids. The procession places the bride and groom in the front of each line. An Okomfo usually leads the processional performing the libation ritual along the way until they reach the to the designated 'altar'.

Special wedding songs are sung during the processional. If either is a priest, their Deity's songs are sung as well as songs for other Deities. If they are Royals, members of the Asafo Company perform, or if they hold other prominent positions, the appropriate songs for those positions are also sung. Ancient rituals to symbolize important elements of marriage are included in the wedding ceremony. The ancient ritual of foot washing is performed as a type of purification of the couple and to denote humility going into the marriage as well as the symbol of clearing all issues of the past to take a fresh, clean step into the marriage. The Best Man and Matron of Honor, or even a family member or a dear friend performs this ritual. After all the rituals have been performed, the couple is declared one and married. Finally, the couple is the first to dance to traditional drumming and songs.

During this time of traditional drumming and dancing, an Akom may begin with the Abusua or village Deities appearance to sanction the marriage. Many of the community members join in the sacred dance to show their support. Of course, there are some family members who have adopted other religions may try to snub this part of the celebration. It is interesting to note that rather than say anything, they just fade away (peeking in periodically) until the display is completed. After this sacred display, a band or DJ begins to play highlife, which signals that the wedding feast and party has begun.

Presently, the newly married couples have the option of having a civil ceremony. This civil ceremony is usually performed in the courthouse at the Justice of the Peace, which ensures that their marriage is registered in the court system. The vows of the civil ceremony are similar to the vows in the US system. An embossed marriage certificate is given to the couple. On the new civil marriage certificate, there is the designated column to report the particulars of the traditional ceremony including the date and place it was held. Thus, both ceremonies are recorded.

In Akan culture, the traditional marriage ceremony involves the family and community who pledge their support to ensure that the couple stays together through the good times and any adversity that should arise. Divorce is absolutely the last option. Elders, family, and community members have pledged to try to keep the family together and are in place to help work out all issues that may arise.

Recently, the civil divorce system was introduced to Ghana. However, the traditional way of doing things pertaining to marriages, even with those couples who claim to be "liberated" from tradition and customs, is still the most prominent system used to settle marital differences.

Marriage is looked upon as the joining of two families to continue the lineage of the family Clan and to carry out the wishes of the Ancestors. If issues arise in a marriage, the Deities are consulted, life force offerings are given, and many types of rituals for Ancestors are done to help restore the health of the marriage. No marriage ends in the Akan culture without exhausting all of the traditional avenues for resolution and reconciliation. And, it is everyone in the family and community's business. Therefore, there are no secrets.

The question of polygamy is constantly raised. Men have the option of having one or more wives as long as they can provide for them. The wives do not usually live together but are housed in another compound. However, the children all know each other and communicate with each other unless the wives forbid the connection. The new wives are brought into the family by a traditional wedding and do not have the option of a civil marriage. Again, the man must go through the particulars described above as well as seeking the consent of the senior wife, which is sometimes given reluctantly. It is the husband's responsibility to keep things straight and to maintain peace among all. Our Ancestors have sanctioned multiple wives and there is no traditional Spiritual objection to such. Even though the traditional ceremony is not a civil ceremony, the recent laws of Ghana have recognized it as 'legal' and have established inheritance laws for all. This works in tandem with traditional customs concerning inheritance.

The question of polyandry, meaning a woman has more than one husband, has occasionally been raised. To date, this type of marriage has not been officially upheld, recognized, nor openly discussed in Ghana.

Designation of Elders

The selection and enstoolment of an elder is based on the same criteria as the Chief and other royals. The difference is that more family members may be eligible for the position based on age alone. The selection of the Abusua Panyin and Obaa/Oba Panyin is done with the same vigor and protocols as with selecting a Chief.

An enstoolment ceremony for an Elder, though not as extravagant as the one for a Chief or Queenmother's ceremony, is performed. An oath of allegiance is administered as well as other rituals to obtain the permission of the Ancestors to continue the process. They newly enstooled is properly introduced to the Ancestors with accompanied rituals.

Enstoolment and Installation of a Royal

This is the epitome of political and spiritual processes in the Akan culture. These ceremonies are also among the most important in the traditional system. Therein lies the fabric and extension of the Akan culture and community.

The enstoolment and installation entails many Shrine and ancestral consultations, council of elder discussions, family discussions and rituals to determine the qualifications of the nominated individual. Sometimes these discussions continue for days on end as many aspects of the individual's character, work ethics, family, marital status, children, overall accomplishments, finances, social habits, business alliances, personal associates and personality are invaded. If there are any secrets, they are put on the table for discussion. If there are alternate candidates comparisons are made to the qualifications of the nominated. This process becomes animated and quite often combative. However, the family makes a decision and that decision is carried out. Often, disputes arise from these decisions.

The selected individual is somehow informed that they will be enstooled. They immediately make themselves scarce as it is up to the Kingmakers to "catch" the person to literally "lift them" to the position. Subsequently, the enstoolment is accomplished. The individual is lifted into the air and customary powder is sprinkled on them as they are carried through the streets of the village passing all of the important Shrines, monuments and houses.

**Enstoolment of
Nana Kwa Kra Whitaker as Tufohene of Atonka Village**

After which, certain rituals are performed and the person is taken into seclusion for the designated period of time. During seclusion, the now enstooled individual is given Spiritual baths and medicine, the elders teach them the duties and responsibilities of their position including the secrets of the position, protocols, taboos, proper dress and comportment, and all the necessary instruction to begin their reign immediately following their installation. They are taught how to perform the traditional dance which is presented by each royal.

During the seclusion, the village is in a waking keeping mode, for this is the burial of the ordinary person to the making of a Royal who is another leader of the village. This person is leaving all of the old loyalty to themselves to take up the loyalty and commitment to the growth and development of the village or family. Thus, there is utter excitement in the air.

The installation is conducted at the end of the seclusion period. This is a very festive occasion in which the public participants are arrayed in their finest attire. The new Royal is dressed in the finest available attire with all the jewelry and implements. Again, they are carried through the streets in a palanquin to show off and finally to the designated place for the swearing in ceremony. The swearing in ritual is comprised of several components including calling the Ancestors, feeding the Ancestors, libation, swearing of an oath to the Abusua Panyin and village, the village pledging allegiance and commitment to the new Royal, there are speeches, gift giving and finally cultural displays and dancing. Family members, village residents, associates, and well wishers travel from near and far to witness the carrying on of the culture.

**Nana Kodwo Eduakwa V, Chief of Atonkwa Village in Installation Regalia (left);
Nana riding in Palanquin after Installation (right)**

Ayie Rites (Funeral Rites)

Each region of Ghana has its own format for burials and funerals. The funeral and the enstoolment are the most important ceremonies in this culture. Why is this? They are the foundation for survival of the members of the community. Ancestral honor and veneration is the basis of Akan religion and culture. Therefore, every Akan expects to have a grand funeral with all the rituals and ceremonies conducted that are required by the family tradition.

The common thread is that the rituals are performed to help the soul of the person who died make the transition from earth back to Nyame. The Spirit travels to the land of the Ancestors, which is called Asamando. It is also a time of making peace with the person's Spirit and gives the family an opportunity to mourn the passing of an important community member. It gives the community an opportunity to honor, show respect and mourn the passing of an important family member. It is also a time of cleansing for the family members and community who are deep into the grieving process that includes wailing and crying. It is one of the rituals that help the community to purify itself from the drastic emotions involved in the loss of a loved one.

As discussed previously, there are certain categories of Ancestors. Each category requires its own special rituals to be performed. For example, if a person is elderly and decides to make transition, certain rituals are performed. If the person is sick and dying certain rituals are performed. If the person succumbs in an accident, certain rituals are performed. In any other types of deaths, appropriate rituals are performed. We are speaking of Akans. Other tribes and religious groups have their own rituals which are more similar than different. One of the major differences would be the burial timing and techniques. Some groups use water rituals, some fire rituals and some a combination of all with one predominately important aspect.

Let us suppose an elderly person is making transition. The family gathers around the person's house and each person is allowed a few private moments with the elder in order to say goodbye, receive messages or otherwise to clear up any questions, problems express love and gratitude or any other form of communication necessary. The person is not expected to do a lot of crying, because this is a time that the elder is transitioning from earth plane to Spiritual plane. This time is to be honored, revered and celebrated. One knows that the transition is being made because the Spirit has completed its mission on earth at this time, and is preparing to take its place in another plane or order to complete whatever works are necessary there. Ultimately, the Spirit may return in another form such as a male or female child. I might add that even though each family member desires to have private time with the individual, there is a core group of family members who keep watch to ensure that nothing inappropriate takes place that sacred space.

The Priest (both traditional and nontraditional) and a Chief, if it is a Royal, enter the room to convey blessings on the Spirit, and to give instructions. Some of such instructions would be begging the Spirit to leave peacefully; to not forget the family members in terms of the work that is needed; to return if possible; and to continue to help the family and community. Sacred rituals are performed in conjunction with this ceremony. Small amounts of water are given to the individual to aid them in making the transition. Sometimes candles are lit to help light their way. A special incense is burned in the area of the room. And other forms of external things are done to make the individual as comfortable as possible. As soon as the person's Spirit has left the body, the individual is bathed, given a sweet traditional burial medicine to send the Spirit on its journey. After this ritual, the body is wrapped and those present are permitted a viewing prior to sending the dead body the morgue or being held in seclusion if being held at the home.

Once the person has transitioned, the rumor goes out to the community that the person has made transition. It is up to the family to confirm the rumor to those mourners who may come to ask. It depends on the status of the person and the wishes of the family to confirm or deny the rumor. Initially, the family will only say that the person has traveled or is on a long journey. Sometimes the family is waiting for the proper hierarchy to be informed. Sometimes they are waiting for important family members to arrive. Even though the body may be taken to the mortuary, the rumor may or may not be confirmed. When it is appropriate, the rumor is confirmed and ritual of outward mourning begins. When this is done, immediately the grieving ritual of the wailing women begins. There are professional mourners in every village who know the dirges, know the mourning sounds, can cry on the spot and generally have the ability to cause a whole community to grieve and mourn outwardly which is also a type of purification. It really is an eerie feeling for those who are not accustomed to hearing these soulful sounds.

I recall April 2004, when I had to bury my mother in our village of Atonkwa, as soon as I arrived with her remains, and put my feet on the ground outside of the car, the wailing started. It startled me because this was to be a private ceremony; however, the mourning women heard that I was on my way and thus began the mourning and wailing from the car all the way to the cemetery and throughout the burial ceremony. It only stopped after the official burial. Let me tell you that any remaining grief that I had harbored during the funeral in the US came out when I heard the wailing. My very soul was caught up with the sounds and the intent of the wailing; so you can only imagine the outcome.

Sometimes a person is not taken to the mortuary but preserved with ancient herbs and medicines. Some have been preserved for years. The late Okomfohema Nana Akua Oparebea was preserved with herbs a couple of months. When she was laid in state, you could see some of the places where the herbs and medicines were applied. The body had not deteriorated at all. In fact, her skin was very pliable and did not look hard. She actually crossed the water in November yet the official announcement was not made until January. By then all that needed to be informed in the Diaspora had been informed and were making travel arrangements.

(Several years ago, I had the honor and privilege of attending a funeral of a Chief who had succumbed more than 2 years before the funeral was held. He had been held in the mortuary while a dispute was being settled. Finally, he had this very elaborate funeral which was attended by many Royals and their entourages, cultural groups, entire communities, and mourners who live abroad. It was a magnificent tribute to the Late Chief. At the end of this section are pictures of that funeral.)

Once the announcement has been made the official mourning begins and around the clock vigil is maintained at the family house. The remains are brought from the mortuary or out of seclusion and placed in the family house at the designated time. Usually, this is done on Friday afternoon. At this time, only the family is allowed viewing of the body in state. Sometime in the evening hours the viewing is open to the public and wakekeeping begins.

Wakekeeping is an all night vigil when mourners and well wishers pass through to view the body. Chief Mourners usually put gifts in the casket to aid the person in their journey to Asamando and to signify their status on earth's plane. These gifts could be non-perishable foodstuffs, jewelry, bottled water, implements, traditional medicines and more. Coins are always placed in the casket to purchase their way at certain points of the transition. Before noon on Saturday a service is held at the cemetery and the body is buried before noon. Of course, for Royals the wake keeping might begin on Thursday and burial done sometime during the early hours of Saturday morning. Burial for Royals is in a secret place that is not known to the general public.

Final Ayie Rites for A Chief

After the burial, the family wears red and black to signify that the individual has been buried and the party begins. There is usually a cultural display, speeches, gifts presented to the family, money is presented, and an abundance of food is served for the guests as well as drinks of all kinds. There is plenty of music and merry making in celebration of the person's life. These funerals are paid for by the family members and community. Until very recently, in the past 4 years, there was no life or burial insurance. Family and community are expected to contribute because, **the ancient Elders say** *"The hoe of death does not weed in one place.* "Attendees are expected to make monetary donations to help defray the expenses of the funeral.

Until very recently there was no funeral insurance. Even though it is now in place, most Ghanaians cannot afford such. Therefore, the ancient system of contributing toward the expense of a funeral is a necessary tradition. As the proverb indicates, by all means, each person will have a death in the family and will need the help of others.

On Sunday morning, the family and well wishers attend a thanksgiving service at the church that the person attended or supported. It is known that those who follow the Akan Akom tradition, do not routinely attend church, however many are know to support a church by giving a significant annual donation during their Shrine's festival. Thus, the thanksgiving service is held at that church. It is sometimes followed by an Akom which is then followed by music and more partying or vice versa.

I have mentioned the soul's journey. Akans believe that the soul of the person goes immediately back to God. However, the Spirit's journey to Asamando takes one year. The first 7 days, it is believed that the Spirit is close to the earth and often visits people and places of their interest. After the seventh day, the journey begins towards the river of the land of the Ancestors. The Spirit crosses the river on the 40th day. On this day, the family honors the occasion in several ways. First, they pour libation to acknowledge the Spirit traveling. Secondly, they attempt to settle all debts left from the burial service and as well as debts left by the decedent. Thirdly, there is a celebration…some big some small. Since it is believed that the soul has reached the land of the Ancestors, people begin to mention their name in libations. On the 80th day, libation is again poured to that Ancestors hoping that all is well and they are settled.

After one year, there are the final funeral rites to celebrate the arrival of the Ancestors in Asamando. It is believed that they now are able to fully assist in the daily lives of those left on earth. Family members are now able to make requests whenever necessary. Celebrations are held periodically to commemorate the Ancestor's transition. At every Akwasiadae, those family and community members who have transitioned are remembered.

One-year funeral rites are performed to honor the decedent and to make certain that they have landed in Asamando and are not still roaming around. Therefore, no other rites need to be performed. This is the time that the spouse and children end their mourning. They are now able to wear regular colors and not limited to funeral colors in public. Sacred rituals are performed. Sometimes a full program is conducted in the same manner as the burial program. Most of the time however it is a scaled down version of the burial service, if the person is not a Royal. The final funeral is a very important event and cannot be skipped for fear of retribution by the Ancestor. The same process for settling final debts is used.

Burials and funerals are very elaborate in Ghana and take a lot of planning and activity to execute. Not to mention the enormous amount of debt it brings on the family. However, despite these facts no family wants the stigma of not giving a proper and befitting burial to one of their loved ones. Not only that stigma is attached, but also they don't want to anger the Ancestors.

Final Funeral Rites are performed for Royals. This must take place prior to the full inheritance of the stool. In other words, the enstoolment of a new Chief following the death of his predecessor is not deemed complete until the final funeral rites have been performed. The new Chief finds this responsibility, obligation and funding *"on his neck."* Additionally, the spouse continues to wear mourning cloth until this final funeral takes place. Sometimes various calamities happen to the family, village, and town until these rituals are performed. It is believed that the decedent is not happy and is demanding that final attention. Also, the community is locked into a certain type of mourning that prevents them from carrying out certain required ceremonies and festivals.

The new Chief tries to make this Final Funeral Rites even more elaborate that the burial rites. This bestows a great honor on the deceased and the family. It also gives the new Chief a favorable reputation with the community. Recently, I attended the Final Funeral Rites of a deceased chief, which was held three years after his burial. This is very fast because sometimes it is 10 years after the burial rites. I had previously attended a final funeral for a Chief who had transitioned 6 years prior.

Following is a partial description of the 5-day ceremony. It is not uncommon for the ceremony to take a full week. Much planning is done prior to the actual event.

Wednesday

The family started to arrive from various towns and villages. They found housing in the village and surrounding villages. The cooks began to assemble the cooking pots, utensils, and food. Things began to take shape. Red Cloth was distributed to those who did not have it. Food was prepared for those who had arrived. A cultural group played fro tom fro drums for several hours to announce the beginning of the funeral. The children were present and a part of the celebration.

Thursday

Early morning sacred rituals were performed for the beginning of the funeral. The family gathers and subsequently parades through the streets with a very large sacred cow in the lead

Some family members and well wishers joined the Chief and his entourage as they paraded the cow through the streets. They were carrying brass pans with gifts of food such as fowls, yams, cassava, plantain, eggs, Palm Oil, cooking oil, tomatoes, onions, garlic, bread, fish. Drinks were also included, such as, minerals, beer, Guinness Stout, Castlebridge gin, schnapps, whiskey, gin, vodka, and water. Some other forms of gifts were cloth, such as red, black, festive cloth, kente cloth; millions of cedis/money; gold implements and jewelry; and much more.

The protocol of the line up was quite orderly and specific. Following the offerings was the processional of Royal family members including the new Chief and Queenmothers, who walked very regally in their mourning, clothe under large traditional umbrellas. The Queenmothers were dressed in Black with Red. The Chief was resplendent in all Red. Each was surrounded by a multitude of family members that included the Abusua Panyin, Asafohene, and Oba Panyin. The streets were lined with mourners and well wishers. As everyone knew that this would be the last days of mourning for the old Chief who was well known and a friend to many. The entourage traveled 5 miles on foot through the streets of the town, passed the family house, important Shrines and houses, the Ahenfiyie which is the Omanhene's palace and back to the village.

After arriving at the village, all participants were served a scrumptuous meal and rested. During the evening, choral groups performed.

Friday

On Friday morning, the family gathered for the sacrificing of the sacred cow. Rituals were performed and the cow was sacrificed in public view for all to see. Again certain rituals were performed.

The evening was filled with music, cultural performances and more. Folks were tired but still able to continue with the program.

Saturday

This was the big day of celebration with elaborate canopies set up, chairs, and a PR system for the program and music. Many many visitors from other villages, towns and regions were in attendance. In addition, elected officials and political appointees were present. This was the day that the final obituary was read. Another highlight of this event was the procession of the Omanhene and entourage of members of the Traditional Council including Chiefs and Queenmothers, who came to pay a final tribute to a dear friend, advisor and colleague. The pageantry was second to none. Certain rituals were performed by the Omanhene to determine if the deceased was satisfied with the event, if he was planning to return and to receive his last message. This was performed in private after visiting the panyinfo Ancestors at the cemetery and at the public gravesite of the deceased Chief.

After this was determined, a public sacred offering was presented and the stool was washed signifying that the new Chief was now officially unencumbered and free to reign without interruption or hesitation. There were many performances, speeches, and cultural groups including the brass band and a very skilled dancer performed the very regal and complicated Kete, which is the national dance of Ghana. All was done with much finesse and splendor. Finally, after a very long day, the day's events ended and everyone was served the cooked meat of the cow and sheep until they were full.

Sunday

Finally, the Roman Catholic Church, under a splendid canopy befitting the occasion, conducted a full mass Thanksgiving Service. Gifts were presented to the church on behalf of the deceased and family. Special prayers were said for the family members.

After the church service, the deceased's matrilineal village and his patrilineal village played a quite competitive soccer match. Following the football match, the Abusua Shrine began the drumming and songs, and an Akom was held in the Akan Akom Tradition.

This was the culmination of the activities for the Final Funeral Rites, which allowed the family and friends to cease the mourning, the widow of the deceased to stop wearing mourning cloth, and the new Chief to gain full control over his village.

Chapter 9

SPIRITUAL SERVICES OFFERED BY AKAN SHRINE HOUSES

Spiritual services conducted in the Akan tradition are in place to heal and assist in successful living. Each Bosomfie or Shrine house has its own specialty in terms of services. However, there is a common thread among the Houses. It is a service house whose duty is to promulgate Akan culture, apply ancient healing modalities to meet the needs of African people, to bring a positive energy to its clients and to provide survival services to the community. These services are provided in various ways by each Shrine House and according to its capabilities. Though each Okomfo is trained to provide the following services, each one has a specialty.

Divination or Psychic Readings

The opportunity to talk with Deities about any issue you need help is provided by an Okomfo. The tools used in divination vary according to the training of the Okomfo and the method that that person's Deity uses to convey messages. In some instances, a Kuru or divination pot is used. Sometimes, shells are used, nature symbols from the earth may be used; beads may be used; and other varied instruments may be used. Divination is psychic and can be auditory, visual, and/or tactile. It is always transported spiritually by the Deities and Ancestors. Thus the Okomfo who is divining must be clean, clear, and concise. This is a very refined process and requires very intense training. Those skilled in the Akan process of divination can use almost any medium to receive messages.

During the divination session, the client may receive direction, guidance and insight on health and family, Spiritual journey, job, career, or more. It is a starting point for other Spiritual work that may be needed. A Shrine Okyeame or Assistant is present to assist the Okomfo, the Deity, and to record the transactions in the Shrine.

Spiritual Bath

A Spiritual bath may be total immersion in water, sprinkling or other method that is used to assist in various aspects of one's life. The bath is made of ancient medicine, herbs and is given in a very specific way that the Okomfo has been trained to do in the Akan tradition. The Spiritual bath can be for protection, spiritual clarity, cleansing, fortification, healing, emotional balancing and more.

House Cleansings

This is a spiritual cleansing of living space that is performed by an Okomfo. Again various mediums are used to clear negativity, unknown Spirits, and to replace them with positive energy, and familiar Spirits such as the Abosom, Spirit guides and personal Ancestors. This is often done when a person moves to a new or different house or apartment. Also, when strange things are happening in the living space, or the space has somehow been defiled, a house cleansing may be recommended. It is recommended that a house cleansing should be performed at least once a year just for protection, peace and harmony in the household. Once a house is cleansed, it is recommended that people entering should remove their shoes in order to lower the contamination of outside Spiritual debris and in honor of the Spirits now residing in the space. Oftentimes, a spiritual talisman prepared by the Okomfo in the Akan tradition may be posted in home for continued blessings and protection.

Medicine and Rituals

Ancient earth formulas are provided for healing and assistance in almost every situation. These formulas were concocted by our Ancestors and continue to be passed down to Okomfo practitioners. In Ghana, there is a group of traditional practitioners called the Ghana Psychic and Traditional Healers Association. This group serves as the umbrella membership for Akomfo and Densini practitioners who use ancient medicines, rituals and formulas. Additionally, the Center for Scientific Research in Plant Medicine which is located in Mampong Akwapim in the Eastern Region of Ghana is currently studying the herbs and formulas used by Akan Akomfo and Densini practitioners and has deemed many of them valid as alternative and complementary medicines for healing mind and body. They are actually validating the Spiritual uses of the medicines as well.

Rites of Passages (Services Provided)

Okomfo are trained to conduct Naming Ceremonies, Weddings, Puberty Rites, Funerals, 40 day rites, memorial services and other rituals to honor certain life and death passages. Any one may contact a Shrine House to procure such a service.

Spiritual Training

Many Shrine Houses provide Spiritual training for individuals who believe they have been called to serve as Okomfo, Bosomfo, Densini and other ordained Akan spiritual professions. Each shrine house has it prerequisites and requirements for one to enter such training. Additionally, many Shrines houses conduct workshops, classes, rituals that are open to the public which introduces interested persons to Akan spirituality, religion, and culture.

Protocol for Visiting a Shrine House to Request Services in the Diaspora

In Ghana, the Shrines or Abosomfie are open and easily accessible. Many are located in housing compounds where shrine residents and assistants live with the Senior Okomfo or Bosomfo. People live there though they may have other jobs. They are the Okyeame, Abrafo, drummers, singers, helpers and Akomfo who make up the Shrine House residents. Husbands, wives and children are permanent residents. In some cases, all the members of the Shrine House may not live in the compound proper but live very close by. This unique arrangement allows for the Bosomfo or Okomfo Panyin to have ready access to a cadre of assistants 24 hours a day. Therefore, a visit to a shrine house for help is merely requires a seeker to walk or ride to the location without announcement and enter. Mobile phones are now available to some Okomfo, however the clients may not have access to the telephone so this method of contact is very seldom used. After Amonee (asking the person's mission) has been performed and libation has been poured, the presiding Okomfo will determine if the work can be done on the spot. If not, the individual is informed that they must return with certain items, or if the client must live at the Shrine compound for a period time to have the prescribed work done, they are told at this time.

In the Diaspora, however, the situation is quite different. Most Akomfo are working outside of the Shrine House and the assistants are working and living elsewhere. This is a function of the society that does not honor the African culture, the Bosomfie, and the administration of ancient Akan traditions. Additionally, the economy dictates that many Akomfo have other jobs in order to support their Shrine Houses. Therefore, in the Diaspora, notice must be given in order to set up the proper situation for a visitor. There may be one or two Bosomfie that operate very close to the Ghana model. In any event following is a model of how to visit a Shrine House in the Diaspora.

First, one must make an appointment with the Okomfo. Usually, this can be done by making a telephone call to the Shrine House. Some Okomfo have attendants to return your call to set up the appointment and to tell you what to bring to the initial visit. Women must be careful not to make an appointment while experiencing her menstrual cycle. This could prohibit entrance to the Shrine or certain work to be done. So it is strongly suggested that the appointment should be made before or 7 days after the cycle.

A visit to the Shrine House requires that you present an offering(s) in the form of a bottle of Schnapps, a litre of drink (gin, scotch, rum), Florida water, and/or powder. Usually an initial knocking fee is also required.

Practitioners should not wear Funeral colors to the shrine house unless the person is actually in mourning. However, anyone who is not an Akan practitioner can wear whatever he or she chooses to the Shrine house. However, they will be asked to remove the accessories, which are not allowed. When entering the actual Shrine room, do not wear or bring eyeglasses, shoes, stockings, socks, watches or other timepieces, or cell phones. You will be asked to remove them.

Some Shrines do not allow recording apparatus in the Shrine. Gold jewelry is not allowed in white cloth Shrines and most Tegare and other earth Shrines. A word of caution: Always speak the truth in the Shrine; the Deity knows the truth. You don't want to get caught lying to the Deity. Some Deities hate liars and will not respond to you if you lie.

Never ask the Deity to hurt or kill someone as this could have serious repercussions on you and your family. It is always permissible to ask for protection.

The Shrine Experience

When you visit the Shrine for the first time, a shrine assistant will brief you on what to expect during the visit with the Okomfo and possibly the Deity. That person will also ask the appropriate questions to determine if you are ready to enter that sacred space. The Shrine assistant will lead you with your offerings to the shrine and introduce you to the Okomfo. The shrine assistant will remain in the shrine with you to assist you, the Okomfo, the Deity, and to record the visit. This assistant is a highly trained and trusted person who is ethically bound to maintain confidentiality.

After the introductions, Shrine offerings are presented. You will then be asked your mission. At that time, you must state your reason for visiting the shrine and whatever services you are seeking. The Okomfo will then pour libation to summon the Deities and the consultation begins. Sometimes the Deity may begin the reading prior to any questions being asked.

The leading of the Deity, who speaks through the Okomfo, or makes an appearance to deal with the client directly, then controls the visit. Messages are given, and work may be prescribed by the Deity to alleviate the problem or concern. The client has an opportunity to ask questions and get clarification of any message. Work that must be performed immediately is performed, such as a Spiritual bath, purification, or some other ritual for healing or successful living. If there is a need to return, this is explained with specific instructions. It is important for the client to follow instructions implicitly. If there is a need to return, then the follow up appointment should not be missed.

It is customary to take a thanksgiving offering of money to the shrine after the request has been fulfilled. None of the money exchanged during this service is payment for the reading, medicine, or advice because all comes from God. No mortal man or woman can pay for that. However, putting down money at the Shrine is an exchange of energy as well as an acknowledgement and appreciation of the time, energy and skills the Okomfo used in doing the work. Akomfo are trained spiritual professionals and are thus worthy of some type of compensation or remuneration.

As previously discussed, in Ghana, the economic situation and set up is much different than here in the Diaspora. The compensation may be in terms of food from the vegetable farm, a pan of fresh or smoked fish from the fishmonger, a sack of charcoal from the charcoal farm, and always with an affordable amount of money. In the Diaspora, this exchange is usually in currency plus items to support the work of the Shrine house. These items consist of candles, Florida water, powder and other gifts for the Deities.

Chapter 10

ADMINISTRATION AND OPERATION OF SHRINE HOUSES

Let me stress to you that each Shrine House has its own organizational structure; some more tightly knit, others more loosely, and free flowing. However, a recurring and dominant theme is order based on Akan culture which requires order. The Abosom and Ancestors speak about, illustrate and demand order. There is good reason for insistence on order. For many hundreds of years, the gods and Ancestors have done things in a particular way. This has led to continuity of the tribe, culture and religion. Their way works because certain actions and results come out of that ritual, that custom, that tradition, that way of doing things, which benefit us even today. We are very fortunate to have the benefit of this ancient wisdom to draw upon and apply to our lives.

Order permeates Akan religion and culture and it begins at the top. In the Akan Spiritual pantheon, there is a distinct hierarchy where everyone has a role. There is a clear demarcation of responsibility. God is always first and supreme. He has unilateral rule over life and death. He has unlimited powers. All others have limited powers as prescribed by God. Then Asase Yaa, Mother of Earth, is next to God for she provides the sustenance to allow earth to continue. The Abosom have a hierarchy, some more popular than others, and powers dispersed as God would have it. The Ancestors of course are an extension of life and therefore are treated as such.

The organization of Shrine houses is similar. After the Ancestors, we come into the order. The Okomfo Panyin has the vision and is the main communication link between Almighty God, the Deities, and the Shrine House members. That person is responsible for carrying out the mission as ordained by God and the Deities. There is a Shrine Okyeame who is a servant to the Shrine and has specific responsibilities including Obrafo work. There is the Obrafo who is responsible for the upkeep of the shrine and all of the sacrifices and implements associated with the Shrines. The Shrine Osofo is an advisor to the Okomfo Panyin on all administrative matters. The Akomfo are servants to their Deity and hold the Okomfo Panyin, their teacher, in the highest esteem. They help maintain the Shrines in ways that only an initiated Okomfo can do. The Bosomkorafo is responsible for the overall appearance of the Shrine House. The Gyegyefo is responsible for the maintenance of the attire and implements of the Deities. The members have various responsibilities according to their abilities and interests.

Most Shrine Houses establish guidelines for members to assist in the upkeep of the Shrine House, rituals and ceremonies. All donations and contributions are strictly voluntary and most often come in the form of services and goods, (i.e. foodstuffs, drinks, candles, et al.) This is the Akan tradition and custom. Most Akomfo in the Diaspora hold full-time jobs in order to financially support themselves, therefore voluntary financial contributions to the Shrine houses are appreciated to help in the upkeep of the Shrines.

Akan Shrine compounds in Ghana are committed primarily to festivals, training and consultations. In the Diaspora, however, Shrine Houses tend to conduct ceremonies, services, programs and events that serve the community. Each Shrine House has its own membership requirements. Most require that you affiliate yourself for several months before a membership is offered. Other requirements must be met as established by each Shrine house. Some houses do not have membership per se but Akomfo that are trained there are considered to be members. Shrine house members receive various Ahenies and spiritual medicines where they are initiated. Usually at least one of those beads identifies with a particular Shrine House.

Various ceremonies and rituals require the participation of all members who have an opportunity to become involved in a deeper degree to the Shrine.

Chapter 11

AFTERWORD

Funtummireku, denkyem funafu;, won yafunu ye biako nso wodidi a, wofom.

ADINKRA SYMBOL

"The Akan symbol for society and it suggests that society is made up of individuals with different tastes and desires, hence the two heads and two tails of the crocodiles, which can be easily identified. Common observation shows that the conflicts which arise in society are largely due to the individuality of its members. But the symbol takes the observer beyond the individuality of members of society to point out the common stomach of the crocodiles. Members of society have something in common and it is that which they have in common that sustains them all. The interest of the members of society is convergent rather than divergent and the cooperation of each member of society ensures the prosperity of all." (Excerpt from Hearing and Keeping Akan Proverbs, Opoku 1997)

The information contained in this book is likened to "the tip of the iceberg". I have decided to stop writing at this point because I realize that I could be writing for many more months while many practitioners and seekers are waiting for the information contained herein. This book is a <u>primer</u> for those who want to know about the Akan religion, rituals and practices. It is often said that Akan culture and religion is an oral tradition. Until recently not much had been written to chronicle our ancient practices. It is only within the last decade, that we in the Diaspora have been trying to share information about the ancient practices and traditions of the Akan religion and spirituality as we are learning it. Most of us were not born on the Continent and did not grow up around the Shrines and we, therefore, are relying on the wisdom of the Elders with whom we are now interacting.

Much of the information continues to be oral and not written because it is proprietary information, shared on a need to know basis. However, I have attempted to leave you with a better understanding of the connections of the

Akan religion, to those of other African religions. This book has also attempted to help give you a better understanding of customs and traditions that we here in the Diaspora have actually been practicing as taught to us by our parents and grandparents. I am sure that in these pages you have been able to say, "ah ha, this is where that came from!" It has been a pleasure to share this significant amount of information with you.

It is my hope that others in the Diaspora who are practicing Akan culture and religion who have been studying in varying degrees since the religion was openly introduced in 1965, will also decide to share their perspectives of the Akan Akom Tradition with you.

Our ancient Ancestors were brilliant. They were able to memorize and recite long passages of important information without error thus the oral tradition was alive and well. Today, with the advent of printed word, television, telephones, and other modern and non-traditional forms of communication, we find ourselves not as dependent on the oral tradition. In almost every profession, school and religion, we are required to gain knowledge through reading passages, volumes, write them down, and then memorize them. Literary orientation has taken over for those of us born and raised in the Diaspora. We suffer the loss of some of that memorization skill.

I believe that we need to get the word out, to the masses, about the benefits of our culture, which have helped us to survive. Unfortunately, we find ourselves in the predicament of needing to adapt the very mechanism that has helped to dull our inherent senses, a system that was actually foreign to our Ancestors. Thus, in the past decade, more people of African descent have been encouraged by our Ancestors to use the modern techniques of disseminating information about our culture. We have been encouraged to write about the culture, the religion, and the practices of the Akan people so as not to lose the information. Limited memorization and oration skills, as a direct result of today's literary orientation, has indeed made it necessary to preserve the tenets of our culture using a form of modern technology, writing. Of course, information that is proprietary, on a need-to-know level, will continue to be transferred in the ancient oral tradition to those who need to know.

We, in the Diaspora, did not grow up with the full understanding of who we really are. Researching Akan practices requires patience, long hours and days, and a knowledge of the language (or an experienced interpreter) in order to interview the elders who are keepers of the culture. I believe that preserving and disseminating certain aspects of Akan culture, as with other African religions and culture, embodies the answer to the many dilemmas that people of African descent who were born in the Diaspora, especially our youth, are faced with on a daily basis. We must share the cultural and religious knowledge in order to create and support the trend towards Spiritual transformation that will lead to overall changes in the individual, the family, and community perceptions, morals and values. This transformation will ultimately lead to higher expectations, self-esteem, self-confidence and an understanding of, as well as pride in, our cultural heritage.

I have included seven (7) study guides to serve as discussion points within your organization, group of friends, or individually. Hopefully this will help you to remember the salient points in the book. There is also a list of references which you may use to enlighten yourself about Akan culture, customs and traditions. In addition, there is a Glossary of Twi words utilized in this book, with which you may not be familiar. I also included an index for readily available reference.

So it is with peace, love, and a sense of fulfillment that I close this edition of sharing. I encourage you to continue studying. Find a teacher. And, if you believe this is your destiny, I challenge you to follow your path.

The ancient Akan Elders say:
"God's destiny assigned to you cannot be changed."

Nana Kyerewaa
December 2004

Chapter 12

Traditional Akan Religion, Rituals and Practices
A Study Guide
General Discussion

1.   What is the connecting theme throughout the book?

2.   When was the Akan religion openly introduced in the United States and by whom?

3.   What is the history of Nana Yao Opare Dinizulu?

4.   What was the purpose of African Deities coming to the Diaspora?

5.   In the Akan tradition, which was the first Deity to travel to the US.

6.   Who is the Mother of Akan Akom Traditionalists in the Diaspora?

7.   Why should African Americans and other Diasporans read this book?

8.   Give the comparisons of various aspects of Akan religion and Spirituality in the Diaspora?

9.   In what year was the Akan Akom Tradition introduced to African Americans in the US?

10. What is the meaning of Akan Akom Tradition?

11. What are the primary operating entities in the Traditional Akan Religion?

12. Describe traditional Akan attire for women, men and children.

13. Who in the pantheon is responsible for reminding Akans to maintain order, ancient traditions and customs in the family, community and as individuals?

Traditional Akan Religion, Rituals and Practices
A Study Guide
Understanding the Principles of the Akan Akom Tradition

1. What is an Akom?

2. What are the components of the Akom?

3. Who is in Charge?

4. What is the order of the Akan Akom?

5. Describe the components of Akan Akom protocol including the taboos.

6. What is the beginning of the Akom?

7. Describe the Akom orchestra?

8. What is the purpose of the Akom?

9. Describe Okomfo possession.

10. Compare the Akan Akom Tradition to a church service or any sacred worship service.

11. Explain the Akan Trinity and compare to the Christian Trinity

12. What is the moving force in the Akan Akom Tradition?

13. What is the protocol for the Akoms?

14. Recite at least two of the songs listed in this book.

15. Describe the Creation story.

16. Describe the Separation story.

17. Discuss the positive views and objections generated in the community regarding the intense "Sankofa" movement of Africans born in the Diaspora.

Traditional Akan Religion, Rituals and Practices
A Study Guide
The Akan Deities

1. Who created the Deities, and for what purpose?

2. Who are considered to be the Akan Deities?

3. What is the responsibility of human beings to the Deities?

4. How do we describe the Deities?

5. Name the first Deities brought to the Diaspora.

6. Name the towns where Shrines for these Deities were placed.

7. Who brought those Deities to the US?

8. Why was this such an important event?

9. Name ten Deities that are popular in the Diaspora.

10. Name the characteristics of each of the ten named Deities?

11. Which Deity is known as a warrior?

12. Who are the Mmoetia? Describe them.

13. How many systems of Deities are named in the book?

14. Describe those systems.

15. Describe the veneration of the Deities

16. Name three special occasions whereby the Deities might display.

Traditional Akan Religion, Rituals and Practices
A Study Guide
The Abosom

1. Who is at the head of the Akan pantheon?

2. When did that Shrine first arrive in America and with whom?

3. Name the Okyeame and Abrafo to the Head of the Pantheon and their duties.

4. Name and describe the first Deity to travel to America.

5. What was the stated purpose of that Deity's arrival in the Diaspora?

6. Who was responsible for bringing the first Akan Shrines to America?

7. Name the first female Shrine to America.

8. Give the relationships of the first 3 Deities arriving in the Diaspora.

9. Describe the character and work of each deity named.

10. Name 7 other Deities that are popular in the Diaspora.

11. Describe the display attire of each deity.

12. Describe the main ingredient in feeding the Deities. Why?

13. Do you know the favorite foods for each deity described in this book? What are they?

14. Name the Deities that appear frequently to believers and non-believers. In what ways do they appear? Describe these Deities, their character, likes, dislikes and how to acknowledge them.

15. Describe your personal experiences with the Deities.

Traditional Akan Religion, Rituals and Practices
A Study Guide
The Nsamanfo

1. Who are the Nsamanfo?

2. How do you know them?

3. Name the 3 types of Nsamanfo. Describe the differences.

4. What is the difference between the Abosom and the Nsamanfo?

5. How do we acknowledge the Nsamanfo?

6. Describe the difference between the familial, community and State Nsamanfo.

7. What is the highest ceremony for Nsamanfo? Describe its components.

8. Describe the intention and components of building a sacred space for the Nsamanfo.

9. Who is responsible for the maintenance and conducting of rituals for the Nsamanfo?

10. Describe the rituals for Nsamanfo.

11. Discuss your own story and experiences with familial Nsamanfo.

Traditional Akan Religion, Rituals and Practices
A Study Guide
Celebrations and Sacred Days

1. Describe the reasons for celebrations in the Akan community.

2. Describe the components of an Akan celebration

3. Who is responsible for planning and executing a celebration in the Akan community?

4. Name three (3) celebrations presented in this book. Describe the purpose, the responsible person, the planning, and the execution of each component.

5. What is the most important component in a Durbar?

6. Is a Durbar a political or social or religious ceremony?

7. What is the most important component in an Enstoolment and Installation of a Royal?

8. What is the purpose of funerals? Who is responsible for the arrangements and ceremony? What are the components? Describe all components of a traditional Akan funeral.

9. How are birthdays celebrated in the traditional Akan family?

10. What is an Akom Kese? Describe the purpose, the participants, and the order.

11. Name the sacred days in the life of an Akan Okomfo.

12. Describe the similarities and differences in an Akan engagement and marriage with that of the same in the US and other places in the Diaspora.

Traditional Akan Religion, Rituals and Practices
A Study Guide
Rituals and Rites of Passage

1. What is the most important ritual in the traditional Akan community?

2. Discuss the reason why this is the singularly most important ritual in the traditional Akan community.

3. Why is a naming ceremony conducted? What is the process?

4. What are Ye Gora Bra Rites? Describe components that you think might be included in such a ritual.

5. What is the manhood training for Akan boys? Who is responsible for this training?

6. Describe traditional Akan engagement and marriage rituals.

7. What is the traditional marriage called?

8. Are they still in effect today with the new laws? Why or why not?

9. What are the requirements for becoming an official Elder in the Akan community?

10. What rituals are performed to induct someone into the Council of Elders?

11. Describe the traditional rituals and format for the rites of passage ceremony for the dead?

12. What is the funeral called in Twi?

13. Discuss the similarities as well as the differences in the planning, execution and family interaction around a burial and funeral ceremony.

APPENDICES

LIST OF EMBEDDED PHOTOGRAPHS
(In the order that they appear in this Book)

Funeral Rites Drummers

Abrafo Guarding New Chief

Obrafohene Proclaiming Appellations to New Chief

Sub-Chiefs and Queenmothers sitting in State at Funeral

Representation of the Crowd of Mourners

The Late Chief Lying in State

LIST OF CHARTS
(as they appear in the book)

Appellations for God

Ancestral Libation

State Sponsored Festivals

General Libation

Akan Soul Names

Akan Sequential Names

Akan Soul Appellations or Nicknames

GLOSSARY OF TWI WORDS

Aberewa	ah'ber ree waa. Old or mature woman
Aboakyere	Winneba deer catching festival
Abosom	ah bow'sum. Plural of Bosom; the Akan lessor Gods
Abusua	ah bu' sue ah. Family
Abusua Panyin	ah bue' sue ah pan' yen. Head of the Family
Adade kofi	ah dad'di koo'fee. Deity of iron and metal
Adae	Festival for the Ancestors
Ahene(ies)	ah hen'nee. Spiritual beads worn by Akomfo (Traditional Akan Priests)
Akan (s)	Ah'kan. Indigenious culture and people of Ghana, West Africa; means first; pure race.
Akokofena	ah ko ko fen' ah. A certain type of sword.
Akom	ah-comb. Traditional Akan religious service.
Akomfo	ah come'foo. Pl. Of Okomfo. Traditional Akan Priests
Akonedi	ah cone' ne dee. Name of an important shrine in Ghana
Akonti	ah cone' tee. Hunter's stick carried by Tegare
Akyeame	Ah Chime' me. Pl. of Okyeame. *See* Linguist
Amannee	ah man'nee. Refers to welcome process; more specifically the inmission inquiry.
Asafo	ah saaf'foo. Warrior tribe
Asamando	ah so maan' do. Abiding place of the Ancestors
Asomdwee Fie	ah soom' gee Fee'-a. Means Peace and Harmony House
Asuo Gyebi	ah sir' juh'bee. River in Larteh.
Batakari	baa' te car ri. Type of garment worn by Northerners
Bodua	bow' du ya. An implement made from sheep or other animal tail. Carried by Royals or Okomfo.
Bosom	bow'sum. Refers to Akan pantheon's lessor gods.
Brekete	bre'ke teh. A type of drum

Dagomba	daw gome' baa. Tribe located in the northern region of Ghana.
Deities	dee'i ties. Refers to both The Abosom and Nsamanfo.
Donno	du' nno. A type of drum.
Duku	du'ku'. A traditional scarf.
Dzemawodzi	gem'ah woo gee. Ga word which means temple or house.
Edin To	eh den' toe. Traditional Naming ceremony for a baby
Entoma	en tome' ma. Traditional African cloth. Also, cloth wrapped and worn in a traditional artistic style
eto	eh'toe. Specific food for the Abosom and Nsamanfo.
Fanti	fan'tee. Tribe of people in the centeral region.
Koto	koo'toe. Stoop or bend low; kneel
Lappas	la' pus. Cloth wrapped in an ancient way to create 1 or 2 skirts.
Larteh	lar'the. A legendary and important sacred place in Ghana
Nana	nah'nuh. Title given to royalty, elders, grandparents, and in Ghana used for Akomfo particularly Akomfo Panyin. Deities' names are proceeded with this title.
Nsamanfo	en saa man' foh. The Ancestors
Nyame	en ya mae. Almighty God
Obosom	oh bow' sum. Refers to a single traditional Akan lessor God
Obrafo	oh braa'foo. Executioner
Odomankoma	oh da mock'oh ma'. The Creator
Ohemma	oh heem'maa. QueenMother
Okomfo	oh come'foo. A traditional Akan priest or priestess
Okomfohene	The Chief of the traditional Akomfo a particular state or region
Okomfo Panyin	oh come'foo. Traditional Akan Senior or Chief Priest of a particular Shrine house.
Okomfowaa	oh come'foo waa. Traditional Akan Okomfo trainee
Okyeame	oh chime'mee. Spokesperson; linguist
Omanhene	oh man'hene. Highest Chief of a state or region
Onyame	Almighty God

Osofo	oh sof' fo. Owner of a Sacred Shrine or traditional stool; a Reverend of a church.
Petia	pet'tia. A type of drum
Saman-twen twen	sah maan'twen twen. A type of Ancestor.
Tegare	tee'gar'ray. A northern Deity who originated in Northern Ghana.
Tofo	tah-fo. A type of Ancestor

REFERENCES

Ackah, C.A.
Akan Ethics. 1988 Accra

Addo, Ebenezer Obiri
Kwame Nkrumah: A Case Study of Religion and Politics in Ghana
1999 Maryland

African Traditional Spiritual Coalition
A Sacred Healing Circle. 2000 Washington, DC

Ampem, Agyewodin Adu Gyamfi
Akan Mmebusem Bi ____ Kumasi

Anfom-Evans, E.
Traditional Medicine inGhana, Practice, Problems and Prospects
1986. Accra

Arhin, Kwame
Traditional Rule in Ghana. 1985 Ghana

Asamoa, Ansa
Classes and Tribalism in Ghana. 1990 Accra

Bannerman, J. Yedu
*Mfantse-Akan Mbebusem Nkyerekyeremu.*____ Tema

Buah, F.K.
A History of Ghana. 1980 Hong Kong

Cudjiw-Ashong, John
Naming Ceremony (The Akan Traditional Way), 1977 Elmina

Dinizulu, Nana Yao Opare
"Nana Says". 1987 New York

Ghana Tourist Board
Ghana, the Land, The People and the Culture.

Ghana Airways Ltd.
<u>Akwaaba-the inflight magazine for Ghana Airways.</u> 1996 Accra

Gyekye, Kwame
African Cultural Values. An Introduction. 1996 Philadelphia.

Gyekye, Kwame
<u>An Essay in African Philosophical Thought: The Akan</u> Conceptual <u>Scheme.</u> 1995 Philadelphia.

Kefele, Kwasi
<u>Healing, Health and Wellness. Spirit and Resistance. Akan</u> Traditional <u>Healing and Mental Health.</u> 2002 Canada.

Knappert, Jan
African Mythology. 1990 Great Britian

Kura, Jane M.
About Girls, 1998 Nairobi

Ladzagla, Mallet Awuku
Comprehensive Notes on 105 Topics. 1980 Accra

Odaaku, Kwasi
Twi, The Spoken Word, 1995 Maryland

Opoku-Ampomah, J.K.
The Asante Kingdom. 1995 Legon

Opoku, Kofi Asare
Hearing and Keeping Akan Proverbs. 1997 Accra

Opoku, Kofi Asare
West African Traditional Religion, 1978 Awka

Opokuwaa, Nana Akua Kyerewaa
Akan Protocol: Remembering the Traditions of our Ancestors.
1997 Washington, DC

Pobee, John S.
Religion and Politics in Ghana, 1991. Accra

Sarpong, Peter Rev. Dr.
    Ghana in Retrospect. 1974 Accra-Tema

Sarpong, Rt. Rev Dr. Peter Kwasi Sarpong
    Libation, 1996 Accra

Tufuo, J.W. and Donkor, C.E.
    Ashantis of Ghana. 1989 Ghana

University of Legon
    The Cape Coast and Elmina Handbook. 1995 Accra

Yankah, Kwesi
    Speaking for the Chief. 1995 Legon

CONTACT INFORMATION

Nana Akua Kyerewaa Opokuwaa is available for speaking engagements, lectures, seminars, training, and consultations. In addition, the Asomdwee Fie (AFSANI) sponsors traditional tours to Ghana, cultural programs, celebrations, and other Akan related as well as community events. Address all inquiries to the attention of the Administrator of AFSANI Institute at the following email address.

AFSANI.org or AFSANI@aol.com

Index

978-0-595-35071
0-595-35071-2

Made in the USA
Middletown, DE
24 April 2022

64703925R00120